A
MEDIEVAL
HOME
COMPANION

Also by Tania Bayard

Sweet Herbs and Sundry Flowers: Medieval Gardens and the Gardens of The Cloisters

Roses of America: The Brooklyn Botanic Garden's Guide to Our National Flower (with Stephen Scanniello)

A MEDIEVAL HOME COMPANION: HOUSEKEEPING IN THE FOURTEENTH CENTURY

Translated and edited by

Tania Bayard

HarperPerennial

A Division of HarperCollins*Publishers*

HarperCollins books may be purchased for educational, business, or sales promotional use. For information please write: Special Markets Department, HarperCollins Publishers, Inc., 10 East 53rd Street, New York, NY 10022.

First HarperPerennial edition published 1992.

Designed by Linda Florio

The Library of Congress has catalogued the hardcover edition as follows:

Ménagier de Paris.   English
    A medieval home companion : housekeeping in the fourteenth century / Tania Bayard.—1st ed.
        p.   cm.
    Abridged translation of: Le ménagier de Paris.
    ISBN 0-06-016654-1
    1. Home economics—France—Early works to 1800.   2. France—Social life and customs.   I. Bayard, Tania.   II. Title.
    TX17.M3913   1991
    640′.944023—dc20   90-55853

ISBN 0-06-092182-X (pbk.)
92 93 94 95 96 AC/HC 10 9 8 7 6 5 4 3 2 1

For Robert

Contents

Illustrations

11

P. 52: Creation of Eve. Detail of a woodcut from a French *Bible*, Lyon, 1521. Rare Books and Manuscripts Division, The New York Public Library, Astor, Lenox and Tilden Foundations.

P. 54: Dogs. Woodcut from Petrus de Crescentiis, *Das Buch von Pflantzung*, Strassburg, 1512. The Metropolitan Museum of Art, Harris Brisbane Dick Fund, 1926. (26.100.2)

P. 58: Woman on horseback. Woodcut from Chaucer, *The Canterbury Tales*, London, ca. 1491. Rare Books and Manuscripts Division, The New York Public Library, Astor, Lenox and Tilden Foundations.

P. 63: Man warming himself before a fire. Woodcut from *Kalender deutsch*, Augsburg, 1484. The Metropolitan Museum of Art, Harris Brisbane Dick Fund, 1926. (26.56.1)

P. 65: Bugs on a bed. Woodcut from *Hortus sanitatis*, Strassburg, ca. 1497. The Metropolitan Museum of Art, Elisha Whittelsey Collection, Elisha Whittelsey Fund, 1944. (44.7.37)

P. 68: Man grooming a horse. Woodcut from Petrus de Crescentiis, *Das Buch von Pflantzung*, Strassburg, 1512. The Metropolitan Museum of Art, Harris Brisbane Dick Fund, 1926. (26.100.2)

P. 71: God consigning devils to Hell. Woodcut from Bartholomaeus Anglicus, *De proprietatibus rerum*, Westminster, ca. 1495. Rare Books and Manuscripts Division, The New York Public Library, Astor, Lenox and Tilden Foundations.

P. 74: Gardener pulling weeds. Woodcut from Petrus de Crescentiis, *Das Buch von Pflantzung*, Strassburg, 1512. The Metropolitan Museum of Art, Harris Brisbane Dick Fund, 1926. (26.100.2)

P. 76: Plant in pot. Woodcut from Petrus de Crescentiis, *Das Buch von Pflantzung*, Strassburg, 1512. The Metropolitan Museum of Art, Harris Brisbane Dick Fund, 1926. (26.100.2)

P. 77: Violet. Woodcut from *Gart der Gesundheit*, Mainz, 1485. The Metropolitan Museum of Art, Elisha Whittelsey Collection, Elisha Whittelsey Fund, 1944. (44.7.15)

P. 79: Cabbage. Woodcut from Petrus de Crescentiis, *Das Buch von Pflantzung*, Strassburg, 1512. The Metropolitan Museum of Art, Harris Brisbane Dick Fund, 1926. (26.100.2)

P. 82: Peas. Woodcut from Petrus de Crescentiis, *Das Buch von Pflantzung*, Strassburg, 1512. The Metropolitan Museum of Art, Harris Brisbane Dick Fund, 1926. (26.100.2)

P. 83: Gardener planting leeks. Woodcut from Petrus de Crescentiis, *Das Buch von Pflantzung*, Strassburg, 1512. The Metropolitan Museum of Art, Harris Brisbane Dick Fund, 1926. (26.100.2)

P. 85: Vine growing through a tree. Woodcut from Petrus de Crescentiis, *Das Buch von Pflantzung*, Strassburg, 1512. The Metropolitan Museum of Art, Harris Brisbane Dick Fund, 1926. (26.100.2)

P. 86: Woman watering rosemary. Woodcut from Petrus de Crescentiis, *Das Buch von Pflantzung*, Strassburg, 1512. The Metropolitan Museum of Art, Harris Brisbane Dick Fund, 1926. (26.100.2)

P. 88: Man carrying a cask. Woodcut from *Gart der Gesundheit*, Strassburg, 1515. Rare Books and Manuscripts Division, The New York Public Library, Astor, Lenox and Tilden Foundations.

P. 89: Man instructing two workmen. Woodcut from Rodericus Zamorensis, *Spiegel des menschlichen Lebens*, Augsburg, ca. 1475–78. The Pierpont Morgan Library, New York. (PML 139)

P. 91: Woman on a bench. Woodcut from *Romant de la Rose*, Lyon, 1503. The Pierpont Morgan Library, New York. (PML 463)

P. 95: Shepherd tending his flock. Woodcut from Rodericus Zamorensis, *Spiegel des menschlichen Lebens*, Augsburg, ca. 1475–78. The Pierpont Morgan Library, New York. (PML 139)

P. 97: Cat and mice. Woodcut from Bidpai, *Directorium humanae vitae*, Strassburg, ca. 1489. Spencer Collection, The New York Public Library, Astor, Lenox and Tilden Foundations.

P. 103: Man testing wine. Woodcut from Petrus de Crescentiis, *Das Buch von Pflantzung*, Strassburg, 1512. The Metropolitan Museum of Art, Harris Brisbane Dick Fund, 1926. (26.100.2)

P. 105: Woman presiding over a meal. Woodcut from Boccaccio, *De claris mulieribus*, Ulm, 1473. The Pierpont Morgan Library, New York. (PML 194)

P. 107: Woman warming herself before a fire. Woodcut from *Romant de la Rose*, Lyon, 1503. The Pierpont Morgan Library, New York. (PML 463)

P. 108: Two women with lectern and wreath. Woodcut from *Romant de la Rose*, Lyon, 1503. The Pierpont Morgan Library, New York. (PML 463)

P. 109: Man on horseback. Woodcut from Chaucer, *The Canterbury Tales*, London, ca. 1491. Rare Books and Manuscripts Division, The New York Public Library, Astor, Lenox and Tilden Foundations.

P. 113: Man cooking. Detail of a woodcut from Bartholomaeus Anglicus, *De proprietatibus rerum*, Westminster, ca. 1495. Rare Books and Manuscripts Division, The New York Public Library, Astor, Lenox and Tilden Foundations.

P. 114: Man with eel. Woodcut from *Hortus sanitatis*, Strassburg, ca. 1497. The Metropolitan Museum of Art, Elisha Whittelsey Collection, Elisha Whittelsey Fund, 1944. (44.7.37)

P. 115: Market scene. Woodcut from Rodericus Zamorensis, *Spiegel des menschlichen Lebens*, Augsburg, ca. 1475–78. The Pierpont Morgan Library, New York. (PML 139)

P. 116: Geese. Woodcut from Petrus de Crescentiis, *Das Buch von Pflantzung*, Strassburg, 1512. The Metropolitan Museum of Art, Harris Brisbane Dick Fund, 1926. (26.100.2)

P. 117: Men milking sheep and making cheese. Woodcut from Petrus de Crescentiis, *Das Buch von Pflantzung*, Strassburg, 1512. The Metropolitan Museum of Art, Harris Brisbane Dick Fund, 1926. (26.100.2)

P. 118: Hen and chicks. Woodcut from Petrus de Crescentiis, *Das Buch von Pflantzung*, Strassburg, 1512. The Metropolitan Museum of Art, Harris Brisbane Dick Fund, 1926. (26.100.2)

P. 120: Caring for a sick man. Woodcut from Bidpai, *Buch der Weisheit*, Urach, ca. 1482. The Pierpont Morgan Library, New York. (PML 21785)

P. 121: Water. Detail of a woodcut from Bartholomaeus Anglicus, *De proprietatibus rerum*, Westminster, ca. 1495. Rare Books and Manuscripts Division, The New York Public Library, Astor, Lenox and Tilden Foundations.

P. 123: Beehive. Woodcut from Petrus de Crescentiis, *Das Buch von Pflantzung*, Strassburg, 1512. The Metropolitan Museum of Art, Harris Brisbane Dick Fund, 1926. (26.100.2)

P. 124: Woman making horseradish. Woodcut from Petrus de Crescentiis, *Das Buch von Pflantzung*, Strassburg, 1512. The Metropolitan Museum of Art, Harris Brisbane Dick Fund, 1926. (26.100.2)

P. 127: The grape harvest. Woodcut from *Kalender deutsch*, Augsburg, 1484. The Metropolitan Museum of Art, Harris Brisbane Dick Fund, 1926. (26.56.1)

P. 131: Man catching birds. Woodcut from Petrus de Crescentiis, *Das Buch von Pflantzung*, Strassburg, 1512. The Metropolitan Museum of Art, Harris Brisbane Dick Fund, 1926. (26.100.2)

P. 132: Rose. Woodcut from *Hortus sanitatis*, Strassburg, ca. 1497. The Metropolitan Museum of Art, Elisha Whittelsey Collection, Elisha Whittelsey Fund, 1944. (44.7.37)

P. 135: Man feeding birds. Woodcut from Petrus de Crescentiis, *Das Buch von Pflantzung*, Strassburg, 1512. The Metropolitan Museum of Art, Harris Brisbane Dick Fund, 1926. (26.100.2)

P. 137: Stag. Woodcut from *Gart der Gesundheit*, Strassburg, 1515. Rare Books and Manuscripts Division, The New York Public Library, Astor, Lenox and Tilden Foundations.

P. 138: Man talking to a couple seated in front of a fire. Detail of a woodcut from Boccaccio, *Decamerone*, Venice, 1492. The Pierpont Morgan Library, New York. (PML 353)

P. 139: Scribe. Woodcut from a French *Bible*, Lyon, 1521. Rare Books and Manuscripts Division, The New York Public Library, Astor, Lenox and Tilden Foundations.

Acknowledgments

For their help and support, I should like to thank the following people: my editors at HarperCollins, Hugh Van Dusen, and his associate, Stephanie P. Gunning, who saw the manuscript through the publication process with unfailing patience and consideration; my copy editor, Margaret Cheney, and proofreader, Pamela LaBarbiera, who skillfully purged the text of errors; my agent, Janet Manus, and her husband, Justin Manus, who provided sound advice, encouragement, and friendship; the staffs of the Department of Prints and Photographs at The Metropolitan Museum of Art, the Rare Books and Manuscripts Division and the Spencer Collection at The New York Public Library, and the Reading Room at The Pierpont Morgan Library—all of whom graciously allowed me to study their incunabula and granted me permission to reproduce the woodcuts; Linda Florio, whose design for the book delightfully captures the spirit of the text; my good friend Edmund J. Campion, associate professor of French at the University of Tennessee (Knoxville), who generously loaned me dictionaries, checked my translation, and made valuable suggestions (though all mistakes are my own); and finally, my husband, Robert M. Cammarota, who read each phase of the translation, edited the text innumerable times, and was a constant source of encouragement. With love and gratitude, I dedicate this book to him.

A
MEDIEVAL
HOME
COMPANION

Introduction

A round the year 1393, an elderly citizen of Paris married a girl of fifteen. Although this in itself was not unusual at the time, what is remarkable is the fact that the old gentleman, knowing his inexperienced young bride would probably one day be a widow, felt it necessary to write her a book of moral and domestic instruction so she would do him credit with a second husband. In so doing, he left for future generations a priceless document that describes how a medieval woman was expected to behave toward her husband, perform her religious duties, conduct herself in society, manage her servants, plant her garden, and care for her household.

The original late-fourteenth-century manuscript of this anonymous treatise is lost. Three copies written in the fifteenth century are extant, however: two of them at the Bibliothèque Nationale in Paris, and one at the Bibliothèque Royale in Brussels. In the inventories of these libraries, the work is referred to as *Le Mesnagier de Paris*, which might be translated as "The Householder of Paris."

In 1846, Baron Jérôme Pichon, under the auspices of the Société des Bibliophiles Français, published an edition of the text based on a study of all three manuscripts, one of which he himself owned at the time. His work is scholarly and includes extensive notes, but it is not up to the rigorous standards of present-day critical editions because he made many changes in the text, in places altering the spelling and substituting his own words.

Eileen Power summed up some of the author's more intriguing passages in one chapter of her *Medieval People*, published in 1924. In 1928, she translated most of Pichon's text and published it under the title *The Goodman of Paris*, which was the first edition of the work in English. Written in a deliberately archaic style, Power's book has a charmingly medieval flavor, but it must be read with the understanding that it is based on Pichon's edition rather than on the fifteenth-century manuscripts.

A fine critical edition of the text, edited by Georgine E. Brereton and Janet M. Ferrier, appeared under the title *Le Menagier de Paris* in 1981. In this painstakingly produced volume, based on years of research, the editors presented most of the medieval text of one of the manuscripts and noted all the deviations that occur in the other

two. They also provided, in English, an extensive glossary and many excellent notes.

I have long felt that the portions of this delightful treatise that reveal details about married life and the management of a household in the Middle Ages should be made more accessible to the general public. In preparing this translation, I have concentrated, for the most part, on those parts that deal with practical matters—the sections that provide for modern readers a picture of an exemplary fourteenth-century household. My translation comprises less than one-quarter of the treatise: only small portions of the author's lengthy discussions concerning worship, chastity, and honor; a great deal of what he has to say about how a wife should care for her husband's bodily comforts; all of his chapters on gardening and the management of the household; most of his suggestions about shopping, cooking, and other practical matters; and a few of his recipes. These are the sections to which twentieth-century readers—who also have to deal with surly workmen, rid their homes of insects, remove stains from their clothes, cure their family's toothaches, and disguise the taste of their stews when they burn them—can most easily relate. Some of the author's solutions to these problems are still valid today. We all know, for example, that we should water the garden in the morning or the evening rather than in the heat of the sun, stir the stew often so it will not stick to the bottom of the pot, and strike a bargain with workmen before, not after, the job is done. This is the kind of practical advice the husband gives his young bride.

I hope the author will forgive me for leaving out a great deal of his treatise. He states in his prologue that he considers the salvation of his wife's soul and the well-being of her husband (either himself or his successor) more important than anything else, and he treats these subjects at length in chapters on worship, chastity, fidelity, and humility, reinforcing his precepts with moralizing tales and biblical examples. As modern readers might soon tire of protracted discourses on the seven deadly sins and their opposite virtues, confession, and the order of the mass, I have omitted most of his sections on religious duties. In deference to modern sensibilities I have also excluded a great many pages in which he stresses how important it is for wives to be humble and obey their husbands. The few passages from these sections that I have retained will give an idea of his tone and show that, while he was thoroughly medieval in his attitude toward women, he was not, as some modern critics have contended, a dictatorial male chauvinist. The examples he gives to prove his points are not one-sided, and he emphasizes constantly that respect and love must be mutual.

With the exception of a few paragraphs, I have omitted the author's section on the care of horses, which is addressed to his steward rather than to his wife, and his chapter on hawking. I have included only a few of his many recipes, since most of them were taken from contemporaneous treatises he had in his library. I have not attempted to convert all the weights and measurements or adapt the recipes for modern cooks. In addition, I have broken his text into sections and given them titles, and in the last two chapters I have rearranged the order of his paragraphs.

Although we do not know who the author of this extraordinary work was, we can deduce certain facts from his text. He was probably between fifty and sixty years of age, a man of experience and learning who owned manuscripts on many subjects and referred to them as he composed his treatise. He belonged to the bourgeois class but liked to give the impression that he was acquainted with people of a higher station in life; he was, in fact, something of a name dropper. He was obviously well-to-do, employing many servants in his house in Paris and on his country estate. Some modern commentators have conjectured that he was connected, in a judicial capacity, with the Parisian government.

As for his bride, whom the husband addresses affectionately as "dear sister" or "fair sister," she was fifteen years old, an orphan from another region, and of a higher social class than her husband. Because she was so young and inexperienced, her husband employed a housekeeper who also acted as her governess and companion. This lady, Dame Agnes the Beguine, belonged to a lay sisterhood, the Beguines, whose members were not cloistered.

Obviously, the author's wife could read. What then must have been her thoughts upon being presented with this tome? Her husband wanted his household to be orderly and his wife to be morally irreproachable, but he makes it clear that he does not intend to place on her shoulders too heavy a burden of duty and obedience. He points out at the beginning of his work that in the early days of their marriage she herself had asked him to help her learn how to conduct herself and manage her household. As he was of a literary and precise turn of mind, he responded by writing for her this carefully thought out and comprehensive treatise. Throughout, he shows an affectionate solicitude for her feelings, often interrupting his moral teaching to assure her that he knows she is virtuous and has no need for the instruction. Nevertheless, he considers himself an expert on everything from comportment to cooking, and he wants to be sure his wife will be equally accomplished in these matters. We cannot know what she felt as she pored over the exhaustive treatise he composed for her, but she must have been touched by the fact that her husband would go to such lengths to help her as she assumed her new duties. His teaching is as kindly as it is sensible, and much of it is as useful today as it was six hundred years ago.

THE MANUSCRIPTS

Paris, Bibliothèque Nationale, Ms. fonds français 12477.

Paris, Bibliothèque Nationale, Ms. nouvelles acquisitions françaises 6739.

Brussels, Bibliothèque Royale Albert Ier, Ms. 10310–10311.

WORKS CITED

Pichon, Baron Jérôme. *Le Ménagier de Paris: Traité de morale et d'économie domestique composé vers 1393 par un bourgeois Parisien.* 2 vols. 1846. Reprint. Geneva: Slatkin, 1966.

Power, Eileen. "The Ménagier's Wife." In *Medieval People.* New York: Doubleday, 1924.

———. *The Goodman of Paris.* London: Routledge, 1928.

Brereton, Georgine E., and Janet M. Ferrier. *Le Menagier de Paris.* Oxford: Oxford University Press, 1981.

LITURGICAL FEAST DAYS CITED IN THE TEXT

When the husband tells his wife what times of the year are best for certain tasks in the garden and kitchen, he often refers to liturgical feast days. The dates are as follows:

The Annunciation of the Virgin Mary	March 25
St. John the Baptist	June 24
St. Mary Magdalene	July 22
The Assumption of the Virgin Mary	August 15
The Nativity of the Virgin Mary (*Septembresse*)	September 8
St. Remi	October 1
All Saints'	November 1
St. Andrew	November 30

The eve (or vigil) of a feast day is the day before.

The Husband's Prologue

Dear sister, because you are fifteen years old, you beseeched me, the week we were married, to be tolerant of your youth and inexperience until you had seen and learned more, and you promised to apply yourself diligently to instruction and to devote all your attention and industry to keeping my peace and love. This you very wisely said (with better counsel, I believe, than your own), entreating me humbly, in our bed, as I recall, for the love of God not to admonish you offensively before strangers or before the people in our household, but to correct you each night, or daily in our room, and remind you of faults or follies of the day or past days, and chastise you if I wished. And then, you said, you would never be remiss in improving yourself according to my teaching and correction, and you would do everything in accordance with my wishes. In this I have taken great comfort. I praise you and am grateful for what you said to me, and I have often since recalled your words.

Know, dear sister, that everything I am aware of that you have done since we were married, and everything you will do with good intent, has been and is sufficient for me, pleases me, and will continue to please me. For your youth excuses you from being very wise and will excuse you again in everything you do with the intention of doing well and not offending me. Know that I take delight rather than displeasure in your cultivating rose bushes, caring for violets, and making chaplets, and also in your dancing and

singing; I wish you to continue to do so among our friends and peers, for it is only right and just that you should thus pass the days of your maidenly youth. Nevertheless, I do not want you to attempt to frequent banquets or dances of very great lords, for that is not at all proper or becoming to your social status or mine.

As for the duties you say you would gladly render me, beyond what you already do, if you knew how or if I would teach you, know, dear sister, that I will be satisfied if you serve me as your good neighbors and relations of our station in life serve their husbands. Therefore, discuss this with them at once and take as much or as little of their advice as you wish. For, knowing you and your virtue as I do, I am not so arrogant that these and all your other services will not suffice for me, as long as there is no guile, contempt, or disdain. I thank you for this, for I realize, dear sister, that your lineage is greater than mine (although that would not protect you, because, by God, the women of your lineage are so virtuous that they themselves, without me, would reprove you severely if they learned of it from me or from others). But I have no misgivings about you; I have complete confidence in your virtue.

Nevertheless, although, as I said, no great service is due me, I want you to know a great deal about virtue, honor, and duty, not so much for my sake, but either to aid another husband if you have one after me, or better to teach your daughters, friends, or others, if you so desire and have the need. The more you know, the more honor you will have, and the more praise there will be for your kinsfolk, and for myself also, and for others around whom you have been raised. For the sake of your honor and love, and by no means to serve myself (for no service beyond the ordinary is necessary for me, even less), and because I have tender and loving compassion for you, who were torn away from your relations and the country where you were born and who for a long time have had neither father nor mother nor any other of your relatives near you to whom you could turn for advice and help in your private needs, except for myself alone, I have many times imagined that I might myself come across some easy general course of study so that you could learn by your own efforts. In the end it seems to me that, if your desire is as you have shown by your good words, this can be accomplished by a general instruction that I will write for you.

I

WORSHIP, DRESS, DEPORTMENT, AND SPEECH

Concerning Worship and Rising

By rising should be understood morning, and morning, in the sense that we are using the word here, means matins. For just as we ordinary people say "day" for dawn to darkness, or from the rising to the setting of the sun, clerics, who pray, say more subtly that this is not the real day and that the natural day, which always has twenty-four hours, begins at midnight and ends the following midnight. Therefore, I said intentionally that morning is called matins because at that time the bells sound to wake the monks and nuns to sing matins and lauds to God, and not because I meant that you, dear sister, or other married women, should get up at that hour. I said it because at the hour when you hear the bell for matins sound, you should praise and pay your respects to our Lord with some salutation or prayer before going back to sleep.

Laziness

One kind of laziness is sensuality. This is the pursuit of bodily desires, like sleeping in comfortable beds, relaxing a long time, staying in bed late in the morning; and in the morning, when one is reposing comfortably, paying no attention, turning over on the other side, and going back to sleep when the bells ring for morning mass. Such lax and idle people would rather miss four masses than a warm sleep.

Prayer to Our Lady

Oh most certain hope, Lady, defender of all those who depend on you, glorious Virgin Mary, I beg you now that in that hour when my eyes will be so weighed down with the darkness of death that I will not be able to see the light of this world, or be able to move my tongue to pray or appeal to you, and my poor heart, which is so weak, will tremble for fear of the devils in Hell and will be so unbearably frightened that all the limbs of my body will dissolve in sweat because of the pain of the anguish of death, you will then, most gentle and precious Lady, condescend to look upon me with pity and help me. Have with you the company of angels and also the knights of Paradise so that by your help the troubling and

terrifying enemies will not be able to have any perception, presumption, or suspicion of evil concerning me, or any hope or power of drawing me away or putting me outside of your fellowship.

Rather, most kind Lady, may it please you then to remember the prayer I make to you now. Receive my soul into your blessed trust, into your care and protection, and into the presence of your glorious Son, to be dressed in the robe of glory and brought into the company of the joyous feast of angels and of all the saints. Oh Lady of angels! Oh Door of Paradise! Oh Lady of patriarchs, of prophets, of apostles, of martyrs, of confessors, of virgins, and of all the saints! Oh Star of Morning, more resplendent than the sun and whiter than the snow! I fold my hands, raise my eyes, and bend my knees before you, most gentle Lady, for the joy you had when your holy spirit left your body without dread and without fear, and, in the presence of angels and archangels, was carried and presented, singing, to your glorious Son, and received and sheltered in eternal joy; I beseech you to aid me and come before me in the hour of such fear when death shall be so near me. Lady, be comfort and refuge for my soul and be disposed to guard it carefully, so that the very cruel enemies of Hell, which are so horrible to see, cannot bring me face to face with my sins. But at your request, let these sins be at once pardoned and obliterated by your blessed Son, and let my soul be presented by you, sweetest Lady, to Him, and at your request be given eternal rest and joy that will never end.

Take Care That
You Are Respectably Dressed

Here I want to speak a bit about clothes. Concerning this, dear sister, if you will take my advice, you will be very careful and pay great attention to our resources and means, in accordance with the social status of your relations and mine, whom you will visit and be with every day. Take care that you are respectably dressed, without introducing new fashions, and without too much, or too little, ostentation. Before you leave your room or the house, first see that the collars of your shift, your petticoat, your frock, or your coat do not overlap, as is the case with some drunken, silly, or ignorant

women, who, not considering their reputation or the propriety of their rank or that of their husbands, go about with gaping eyes, heads appallingly elevated, like a lion, their hair sticking out of their headdresses, and the collars of their shifts and dresses over-lapping—walking mannishly and conducting themselves before people indecently and without shame. When one speaks to them about this, they plead that they are earnest and humble, and say they are so diligent, industrious, and obedient that they pay no attention to themselves. But they lie. They are so concerned with themselves that in respectable company they would not want to have less homage than wise ladies equal to them in lineage, or have fewer obeisances, bows, honors, or lofty speeches than the others—rather, more. Yet they don't deserve this, since they don't know how to protect the honor of their own position or even that of their husbands and their families on whom they bring dishonor. So take care, fair sister, that your hair, your cap, your kerchief, your hood, and the rest of your attire are neatly and simply arranged, so that no one who sees you can laugh at you or mock you. Instead, you should be to all the others an example of order, simplicity, and decorum.

If You Do This,
Honor Will Result

When you go to town or to church, you should be accompanied by companions suitable to your social position and especially by respectable women. Avoid questionable associates, and never go near a suspicious woman or allow one in your company. Keep your head straight, your eyelids decently lowered and motionless, and your gaze eight feet directly in front of you and on the ground without looking around at any man or woman to the right or left, or looking up, or shifting your gaze unsteadily from place to place, or laughing, or stopping to talk to anyone in the street. And if you have come to church, pick a spot that is private and solitary, before a beautiful altar or statue, take your place, and stay there without changing position or moving about. Keep your head straight and your lips always moving in prayer. Also, keep your eyes constantly on your book or on the face of the statue, without looking at any man, woman, painting, or anything else, and without sanctimony or artifice. Have your mind on heaven and pray with all your heart, and in this spirit hear mass every day and go often to confession. If you do this, and persevere, honor will result, and everything good will come to you.

What is written above ought to be enough for a start, for the honorable women with whom you associate (the worthy examples you will take from their deeds as well as their teaching), the good, wise, and honest old priests to whom you confess, and the innate good sense God has given you will guide you and provide the rest.

Many Perils Come from
Talking Too Much

Y ou should keep silent, or at least speak moderately and be discreet, in order to protect and conceal your husband's secrets. Concerning this, dear sister, know that anyone who gets overheated in speaking does not have sound judgment. Knowing how to hold one's tongue is a sovereign virtue. Many perils come from talking too much, especially when one speaks with people who are arrogant or high-spirited, or with courtiers or noblemen. Above all, take care not to speak with such people, and if by chance such people speak to you, you will show good sense if you avoid them and leave them discreetly and courteously. It is absolutely necessary to do this, for even though your heart is sick, you must sometimes master it, and one who cannot do this is not wise. There is a country proverb that says: Anyone who cannot control himself is not worthy of having mastery or authority over others.

In this matter, and in all others, you should be the ruler of your heart and your tongue, so that they are subject to your good sense. Always consider before whom and to whom you speak. I pray and advise you to refrain from speaking too much, whether it be in company or at table. It is not always possible to prevent an unfavorable interpretation of an abundance of words, and sometimes one says in jest and fun amusing words that are afterward taken and repeated elsewhere with great derision and mockery of those who said them. And so, be careful before whom and about what you speak, no matter what the topic of conversation, and what you say, say pleasantly and simply. In speaking, pay attention that nothing comes out that ought not to come out, and that the bridle is in your mouth to hold in the excess.

Be a good confidante, and always remember to keep your husband's secrets. First, even without his knowledge, hide and conceal his misdeeds, faults, or sins, if you know of any, so that he will not be ashamed. For you will hardly find a man who, if he has a friend who perceives his sin, will not then regard this friend less lovingly than before and be ashamed and afraid of him. And so, I advise you never to reveal to others, no matter how intimate you are with

them, what your husband says to you in secret. And overcome the nature of women, which is such, so it is said, that they can hide nothing.

When women tell each other something, the last always adds more, putting something of her own into it and increasing the falsehood, and the next adds even more. Apropos of this, there is a country tale of a good woman who used to rise early. One day she didn't get up as early as usual. Her friend thought that she was ill, went to her bedside, and asked her many times what was wrong. The good woman, who was ashamed to have dawdled so long, didn't know what to say except that she was very drowsy, and in such a way that she was not able to tell about it. The busybody begged and cajoled her, out of affection, to tell, and swore, promised, and vowed that what she said would never for anything in the world be revealed to any living creature—father, mother, sister, brother, husband, confessor, or anyone else. After this promise and oath, the good woman, who didn't know what to say, told her by chance that she had laid an egg. The gossip was amazed, and seemed to be very distressed, and swore more vigorously than before not to utter a word.

Shortly afterward, this gossip left and going home met another busybody who provoked her to say where she came from; and right away she said that she had just visited the good woman who was sick and had laid two eggs. She beseeched her, and likewise the other promised, to keep it a secret. The other met another and in secret told her that the good woman had laid four eggs. The other met another and told her eight eggs; and thus the number increased more and more. The good woman got up, and throughout the town people were saying that she had laid a basketful of eggs. So she realized what bad confidantes women are. And what is more, the story always gets worse right away.

Dear sister, know how to hide your secrets from everyone except your husband, and this will be good judgment. Do not think that someone else will hide for you that which you yourself have not been able to conceal. Be secretive and discreet with everyone except your husband. For you should conceal nothing from him, but tell him everything, and he should also tell you everything. . . . You two, man and woman, ought to be as one, and at all times and in all places the one should act on the other's advice. This is how good and wise people act and ought to act.

II

CHASTITY

A Man Can Have No Better Treasure
Than a Wife
Who Is Virtuous and Wise

You must keep yourself continent and live chastely. I am certain that you do so, and I have no doubt about this, but because I am aware that after you and me this book will fall into the hands of our children or our friends, I willingly record everything I know and say that you also ought to teach your friends and especially your daughters. Tell them, fair sister, it is certain that all good things forsake a girl or woman who is found wanting in virginity, continence, and chastity. Nothing—neither riches, beauty, wisdom, high birth, nor any other asset—can erase talk of the contrary fault, especially if it is once committed or even merely suspected. Because of this, many women of integrity have refrained from the act—and more especially, the suspicion—expressly for the sake of being known to be virgins.

Certainly, a man, no matter what his position, noble or not, can have no better treasure than a wife who is virtuous and wise. Anyone can know and prove this if he chooses to look at the actions, behavior, and good works of the glorious women of the time of the Old Law—like Sarah, Rebecca, Leah, and Rachel, the wives of the great patriarchs Abraham, Isaac, and Jacob, who is called Israel—who were all pure and lived chastely and continently.

Riches, beauty of body and face, lineage, and all the other virtues are cast away and brought to nothing in a woman who sustains blemish or suspicion against one of these virtues. Really, in this

45

case, all is lost and obliterated, all is fallen and can never be restored, the moment a woman has only once been suspected or made the subject of a rumor to the contrary. Even supposing that the rumor is false, it can never be erased. See in what endless danger a woman puts her honor, and the honor of her husband's family and her children, when she doesn't keep clear of the talk that arises from such blame, which is easy to do.

Concerning this, it is worth noting, as I have heard said, that when the queens of France are married, they never read sealed letters unless they are written in their husband's own hand. They read these letters in private; for others they call companions and have other people read them in front of them. They often say they really don't know at all how to read letters or handwriting other than that of their husbands. This is done as the result of good teaching and very great virtue, solely to avoid talk and suspicion, since there is no fear of the actual deed. And since honorable ladies of such high standing do this, humble women, who also very much need the love of their husbands and a good name, ought to do so as well.

Thus I advise you to receive confidential love letters from your husband with great joy and reverence, read them in private, and in private answer him in your own hand, if you know how, or in the hand of another very discreet person. Write back kind and loving words, and tell him about your joys and pastimes. Do not receive or read any other letters unless they are read in public by others, and do not write to any other person unless someone else does it for you.

They also say that queens, after they are married, never kiss a man—neither father, brother, nor relative—except the king, as long as he lives. Why they refrain from this, or whether it is true, I do not know.

This is enough to give you in this section, dear sister. These things are offered more for the telling than as teaching. It is no longer fitting to instruct you in this matter for, thank God, you are and will be well protected from this danger and suspicion.

III

LOVE

When Two Good
and Honest People Are Married

I believe that when two good and honest people are married, all other affections, except their love for each other, are withdrawn, annulled, and forgotten. It seems to me that when they are together they look at each other more than they look at others, they come together and embrace each other, and they would rather talk and communicate with each other than with anyone else. When they are separated, they think of each other and say in their hearts: "This is what I will do, this is what I will say, this is what I will ask him when I see him again." All their special pleasures, greatest desires, and perfect joys are in pleasing and obeying each other. But if they don't love one another, they have no more than a routine sense of duty and respect for each other, which is not enough between many couples.

Be Very Loving
and Intimate with Your Husband

You ought to be very loving and intimate with your husband, more than with all other living creatures; moderately loving and intimate with your good and nearest kinsfolk and your husband's kinsfolk; very distant with all other men; and entirely aloof from conceited and idle young men who have more expenses than income, and who, without property or good lineage, go dancing; and also distant from courtiers of very great lords. Moreover, have nothing to do with men and women who are said to lead corrupt, amorous, or dissolute lives.

Concerning what I have said about being very loving to your husband, it is certainly true that every man ought to love and cherish his wife, and every woman should love and cherish her husband: for he is her beginning. I can prove this, for it is found in the second chapter of the first book of the Bible, called Genesis, which says that when God had created heaven and earth, ocean and air, and all things and creatures in their adornment and perfection, he brought all creatures that had life to Adam, who named each as he liked, and so they are still called. But there was no creature that was like Adam or suited to give him help and com-

panionship. And so then God said: "It is not good for man to be alone. I will make him a helper who is similar to him." Then God put Adam to sleep. He took one of Adam's ribs and filled with flesh the place He took it from, as Moses says in the second chapter of Genesis. (The author of the *History of the Bible*, and Josephus as well, said that God also took some flesh with the rib.) And God made the rib He had taken into a woman. (The *History of the Bible* says He made flesh from the flesh He took with the rib, and bone of the rib.) When He had given it life, He took it to Adam so he

could give it a name. When Adam looked at it, he said: "This is bone of my bone and flesh of my flesh. She shall be called *virago*, that is to say, made from man." This was her first name; and after they had sinned, she was called Eve, which is equivalent to *vita*, for all human creatures that have lived since and will live come from her. Then Adam said: "For this a man shall leave his father and mother and cling to his wife, and they shall be two in one flesh."

That is to say that the blood of the two, the woman and the man, will be made one flesh in the children that will be born of them. This God did, and first instituted marriage, as the historian says. For he said in joining them: "Increase and multiply and fill the earth."

So I say, for the reasons given, taken from the Bible, that a woman ought to love her husband very much since she was made from the rib of the man.

To demonstrate further what I said before, that you ought to be very private and loving with your husband, I give you the rustic example that even the birds of the forest and the tame and savage beasts, indeed predators, have the wisdom and aptitude to practice this. For the female birds follow and stay close to their males and not others, and they follow and fly after them and not after others. If the males stop, so do the females, and they sit close to them. When their males fly away, they go too, side by side. Even wild birds and birds of prey—ravens, crows, owls, sparrow hawks, male falcons, female goshawks, and the like—that are raised from the beginning by strangers, love these strangers more than others since they have taken food from them. It is the same with wild beasts, tame animals, and even beasts of the field.

With domestic animals you see that a greyhound, a mastiff, or a small dog—whether walking in the street, eating, or sleeping— always stays close to the one from whom he gets his food and avoids, and is reserved and timid with, everyone else. If the dog is far away from his master, he always has his heart and his eye on him. Even if his master beats him and throws stones at him, he follows him nevertheless, wagging his tail; and he appeases his master by lying down before him and follows him by rivers, woods, thieves' dens, and battles.

Another example can perhaps be taken from the dog Macaire, who saw his master being killed in a wood and after he was dead did not leave him, but lay down near the dead man, and by day even went far away to seek food, which he carried back in his mouth without eating it—sleeping, drinking, and eating near the corpse— guarding the body of his master, quite dead in the woods. Later, the same dog attacked and several times fought the man who had killed his master. Every time he found him, he attacked and fought him, and finally he defeated him on the field on the island of Notre Dame at Paris. Traces of the battlefield are still there.

By God, I saw at Niort an old dog that lay on the grave where his master, who had been killed by the English, was buried. The Duc de Berry and many of his knights were brought there to see the

marvel of the loyalty and love of the dog that day and night would not leave the grave of his master. The Duc de Berry provided him with ten francs, which were given to a neighbor to obtain food for him for the rest of his life.

It is the same with the beasts of the field. You see it with a sheep and a lamb, who follow and are friendly with their masters and mistresses and with no others. Also wild beasts that are by nature not tame—like wild boars, stags, and does—follow after and keep close to their masters and mistresses and avoid all others.

Likewise, savage beasts that are voracious and predatory—like wolves, lions, leopards, and the like, who are fierce, proud, cruel, ravenous, and rapacious—follow, serve, and are friendly with those from whom they get their food and whom they love, and they are distant with others.

Now you have seen many varied and strange examples, of which the last are real and visible to the eye. By these illustrations you see that the birds of the sky, the tame and wild beasts, and even predatory animals have the wisdom to love completely and be gentle with their protectors and those who are good to them, and to be distant with others. Therefore, for better and stronger reason, women, to whom God has given natural wisdom and legitimate duties, ought to have perfect and solemn love for their husbands. And so I beg you to be very loving and intimate with your husband, whoever he may be.

How Good Wives Act toward Their Husbands, and Good Husbands toward Their Wives, When They Go Astray

Husbands ought to hide and conceal the follies of their wives and lovingly protect them from future mistakes, as did an honorable man of Venice.

In that city there was a married couple with three children. As the wife lay on her deathbed, she confessed, among other things, that one of the children was not her husband's. The confessor at length told her that he would seek advice about how to counsel her and return. This confessor went to the doctor who was looking after her and asked the nature of her illness. The doctor said that she would not be able to recover from it. Then the confessor went to her and told her that he didn't see how God would give her salvation unless she begged her husband for forgiveness for the wrong she had done him. She summoned her husband; had everyone removed from the room except her mother and her confessor, who placed her, and held her, on her knees on the bed; and before her husband, with folded hands, humbly begged pardon for having sinned in the law of his marriage and having had one of her children with another man. She would have said more, but her husband cried out: "Stop! Stop! Stop! Don't say anything else." Then he kissed her and pardoned her, saying: "Say no more. Don't tell me or anyone else which of your children it is; for I want to love each as much as the other—so equally that you will not be blamed during your lifetime or after your death. For through your blame, I will be dishonored, and because of it, your children, and others through them—that is, our relations—will receive vile and everlasting reproach. Therefore, don't say anything. I don't want to know any more. So that no one can ever say that I do wrong by the other two, whichever it is, I will give him in my lifetime what would come to him under our laws of succession."

So, dear sister, you see that the wise man bent his heart to save his wife's reputation, which would affect his children. This shows you what wise men and women ought to do for each other to save their honor.

Here is another example concerning this. There was a great, wise man whose wife left him to go to Avignon with another, young, man. This young man, when he had had enough of her, left her, as such young men often do. Then, because she was poor and desolate and didn't know how to live, she became a common woman. Later, her husband found out about it, was very upset, and remedied the situation as follows: he put two of his wife's brothers on horses, gave them money, and told them to go and search for their sister who was a common woman in Avignon. They were to clothe her in coarse cloth and cockle shells like pilgrims coming from St. James, have her adequately mounted, and send her to him when she was one day away from Paris. They started out immediately. The wise man let it be known publicly that he was overjoyed that his wife was returning home in good health from the place where he had sent her, thanks be to God. When people asked where he had sent her, he said that he had long ago sent her to St. James of Compostela on a pilgrimage with which his father, on his deathbed, had charged him. Everyone was astonished at this, in light of what had previously been said of her. When his wife was a day away from Paris, he decorated his house with leafy branches and green herbs, and gathered together his friends to go to meet her. He went ahead, they kissed each other, and they began to cry and then be very joyful. He bade his wife speak to everyone cheerfully, nobly, and boldly—especially the servants—and when she got to Paris to go to all her neighbors, one after the other, and appear joyful. Thus the good man restored and preserved his wife's honor.

By God, if a man keeps his wife's honor and a wife casts blame on her husband, or allows others to cast blame on him, either secretly or openly, she herself is to be blamed, and justly so. For he is either wrongly or rightly accused. If he is wrongly accused, then she should fiercely avenge him. If he is rightly accused, she should graciously protect and lovingly defend him. For certainly if the blame is not wiped away, she will be considered as bad as her husband and share in the blame because she is married to such a wicked person. For as one who plays chess holds his piece in his hand for a long time before setting it down, while he considers the best place to put it, so should a woman hold back so she can consider, select, and put herself in a good place. If she doesn't do this, then she should be reproached and ought to share the responsibility with her husband. If he is tainted in some way, she should conceal and hide it with all her might. Her husband ought to do the same for his wife, as I said above. . . .

I knew a very renowned lawyer in court who had with a poor woman a daughter, whom she put with a foster mother. Because he didn't pay, visit, or perform other courtesies about which men are ignorant in these situations with foster mothers, people talked and his wife found out about it. She also discovered that I knew about it and was making the payments for this foster·care, to save the honor of the nobleman, to whom I was, and am, much beholden, God save him! Because of this, the wife of this lawyer came to me and told me that I was greatly at fault, for her husband was slandered and defamed. She said she was more obligated than I to bear the difficulty of this care, and that I should take her to the child. She put the child in the custody of a seamstress, had her taught her trade, and then had her married in such a way that her husband never suspected it by any ill will, or by a single angry or ugly word. And this is how good wives act toward their husbands, and good husbands toward their wives, when they go astray.

IV

HOW TO CARE
FOR A HUSBAND

Cherish Your Husband's
Person Carefully

Dear sister, if you have another husband after me, be aware that you must take very good care of his person. For generally when a woman has lost her first husband and marriage, it is hard for her, depending on her social status, to find a second who is to her liking, and she remains forsaken and helpless for a long time, and even more so when she loses the second. Therefore, cherish your husband's person carefully.

I entreat you to keep his linen clean, for this is up to you. Because the care of outside affairs is men's work, a husband must look after these things, and go and come, run here and there in rain, wind, snow, and hail—sometimes wet, sometimes dry, sometimes sweating, other times shivering, badly fed, badly housed, badly shod, badly bedded—and nothing harms him because he is cheered by the anticipation of the care his wife will take of him on his return—of the pleasures, joys, and comforts she will provide, or have provided for him in her presence: to have his shoes off before a good fire, to have his feet washed, to have clean shoes and hose, to be well fed, provided with good drink, well served, well honored, well bedded in white sheets and white nightcaps, well covered with good furs, and comforted with other joys and amusements, intimacies, affections, and secrets about which I am silent. And on the next day fresh linen and garments.

Indeed, dear sister, these favors cause a man to love and desire the return home and the sight of his good wife, and to be reserved with others. And so I advise you to comfort your second husband on all his homecomings, and persevere in this.

Also keep peace with him. Remember the country proverb that says there are three things that drive a good man from his home: a house with a bad roof, a smoking chimney, and a quarrelsome woman. Dear sister, I beg you, in order to preserve your husband's love and good will, be loving, amiable, and sweet with him. Do for him what the good, simple women of our country claim people have done to their sons when they are enamored elsewhere and they cannot get them back. There is no question that when stepsons lose their fathers and mothers and have quarrelsome stepfathers and stepmothers who rebuke and reject them and have no regard for how they sleep, eat, or drink, or for their shoes, shirts, or other needs and concerns, these children find good shelter elsewhere and

the support of some other woman who gives them a new home and sees that they are warm with her by some meager fire, keeps them clean, and mends their hose, breeches, shirts, and other clothes. These children follow this woman, and they desire her company and want to sleep and be couched between her breasts. They are completely estranged from their mothers or fathers, who formerly paid no attention to them and now want to bring them back and have them again. But this may not be, for these children would rather have the company of strangers who provide for them and care about them than that of their relatives who did not esteem them and who now bray and cry and say that these women have bewitched their children and that they are under a spell, cannot leave them, and are not content if they are not with them. This is not sorcery, no matter what they say. The only enchantment is in the love, kindness, closeness, joy, and pleasures these women show them in all ways. For whoever gives all its pleasures to a bear, a wolf, or a lion, that same bear, wolf, or lion will follow him. And, in the same way, the other beasts, if they could talk, might say that those beasts tamed in this way are bewitched. By my soul! I believe doing good is the only enchantment, and one can no better bewitch a man than by giving him what pleases him.

Therefore, dear sister, I pray you to bewitch and bewitch again the husband whom you will have, preserve him from a badly cov-ered house and a smoky chimney, and be not quarrelsome with him, but be sweet, amiable, and peaceful. Mind that in winter he has a good fire without smoke, and that he is well couched and covered between your breasts, and there bewitch him.

Take Care That There Are No Fleas in Your Room or in Your Bed

In summer, take care that there are no fleas in your room or in your bed. I have heard that there are six ways you can do this. Some people say that if you spread alder leaves about the room, the fleas will stick to them. Also, I have heard it said that if at night you have around the room one or more trenchers smeared on top with

birdlime or turpentine, and with a candle burning in the middle, fleas will stick and be caught. I have tried another method and it works: take unfinished cloth, spread it around the room and over your bed, and all the fleas that jump onto it will stick there so that you can remove them with the cloth and take them where you want. Also, sheepskins. In addition, I have seen white cloth put on the covering and the bed, and when the fleas, which are black, jump on it, they are easily seen against the white and can be killed. But the best method is to be on guard against those that are in the covers, furs, and the clothing one wears. I have tried having the covers, furs, and clothes that have fleas in them shut up and enclosed, as in a trunk that is securely tied with straps or in a sack that is well tied and flattened or otherwise compacted, so that the fleas are in a compressed space without light or air, and in this way they instantly succumb and die.

I have seen rooms laden with mosquitoes, which, drawn by the vapors of a sleeper's breath, sit on his face and sting so fiercely that he is forced to get up and light hay to make smoke so they will die if they don't fly away. One can do this in the daytime, too, if he suspects there are mosquitoes. Also, one can protect himself well with a mosquito net if he has one.

If you have a room or a house where many flies gather, take little bunches of ferns, tie them together, shred them at the edges, and hang them up: all the flies will lodge on them in the evening. Then take down these fringes and throw them away.

In the evening, close up your room well, so that there is only a little hole in the wall toward the east. As soon as dawn breaks, all the flies will go out through the hole, which should then be closed up.

Take a dish of milk and a hare's gall and mix them together; then put two or three dishes of this in places where the flies settle, and all those that taste it will die.

Fasten linen cloth to the bottom of a pot that has a hole in the base. Put this pot in a place where flies gather, and smear the inside with honey, apples, or pears. When it is thoroughly full of flies, put a trencher over the mouth and shake it.

Take raw red onions, crush them, squeeze the juice into a dish, put the dish where flies congregate, and all those that taste it will die.

Have paddles for killing them by hand.

Have limed twigs on a basin of water.

Have your windows so tightly sealed with waxed cloth, parchment, or something else, that no fly can get in. The flies that are inside may be killed with the paddle, or by one of the methods described above, and no others will come in.

Have a hanging cord soaked in honey: the flies will settle on it. In the evening let them be caught in a sack.

Finally, it seems to me that flies will not settle in a room where there are no covered tables, benches, cupboards, or other things on which they can light and rest. For if they have nothing except flat walls to grip, they won't settle at all. Nor will they stay in a place that is dark or wet. So it seems to me that if a room is well dampened, well closed, and well sealed, and if nothing is left lying on the plate, no fly will settle there.

Shield Your Husband
from All Troubles

Thus protect and shield your husband from all troubles, give him all the comforts you can think of, wait on him, and have him waited on in your home. You can depend on him for outside matters, for if he is good, he will take even more trouble and pains with these than you could wish. If you do what is said here, he will always have his affection and his heart turned toward you and your service, and he will forsake all other homes, all other women, all

other help, and all other households. All will be as dust to him compared to you, who will take care of him as I have said, and who should do this following the example of horsemen the world over, who as soon as they are at home from a journey give their horses clean litter up to their stomachs. These horses are unshod, bedded down, and groomed; they have choice hay and crushed oats; and they are better treated at home on their return than in any other place. If horses are made comfortable like this, there is all the more reason why the same should be done for people, especially lords, at their own expense, when they return home. When dogs come in from the woods and the hunt, they have clean bedding—made even by the master himself—before the fire. Their feet are anointed with soft tallow, sops are prepared for them, and they are made comfortable out of consideration for their labor. Similarly, if women do for their husbands what men do for their horses, dogs, donkeys, mules, and other beasts, certainly all other houses where their husbands have been waited on will seem to them only gloomy prisons and alien places compared to their own, which will then be for them a paradise of tranquillity. And so, on the road, husbands will think of their wives. No toil will be onerous to them because of the trust and love they will have for their wives, whom they will desire to see again as the poor hermits, penitents, and abstinent monks desire to see the face of Jesus Christ. Nor will these husbands, thus cared for, ever want another home or other company; instead, they will be wary, reticent, and hesitant concerning these things. Compared to their homes, all the rest will seem like a bed of stones. But let this be constant and done with a good heart and without sham.

Be Dutiful

There are some old women who are devious: they pretend they are sensible and feign great love by the appearance of obedience in their hearts, and nothing else. Know, dear sister, that husbands are foolish if they don't perceive this. And if they see it, and the husband and the wife say nothing and dissemble with each other, this is a bad beginning, and a worse end follows.

There are women who serve their husbands very well at first; then they think that their husbands, whom they perceive to be good-natured and enamored of them, will scarcely dare to be angry with them if they do less, slack off, and try, little by little, to be less respectful, helpful, and obedient. What is more, they assume authority, command, and control—first in a small matter, then in a larger one, and then a little every day, bit by bit. And so they strive, get ahead, and advance (or so they think), imagining that their husbands, since they tolerate it in this way, don't see it a bit because they are so affable (or perhaps they are cunning) and keep silent. Certainly this is not a good way to think or act. For when the husbands see that their wives cease being dutiful and gain too much power, and that no good will come from enduring their actions, these women are, all of a sudden, by the rightful will of their husbands, cast down like Lucifer, who was lord of the angels of Paradise. Our Lord loved him so much that He looked the other way and let him do as he wished. Lucifer swelled up, grew more arrogant, did so much, and attempted so much more, that he overreached, went too far, and angered our Lord, who had for a long time dissembled and endured without saying a word. Then all of a

sudden remembering, He cast him down into the deepest part of Hell because he did not continue the appointed service for which he had in the beginning gained our Lord's great love. Therefore, you should be dutiful in the beginning and always abide by this precedent.

V

GARDENING

Rainy Weather
Is Good for Planting

Sow, plant, or graft in damp weather, at the waning of the moon, and in the evening or early morning before the heat of the sun. Water the base of the plant and the earth, not the leaves.

Water in the evening, never when the sun is hot. In the morning do not cut cabbage, parsley, or other plants that send out young shoots, for the heat of the sun will bake the cut and burn it so that no new shoots will grow from this point.

Rainy weather is good for planting, but not for sowing seed, for the seeds will cling to the rake.

December, January,
February, and March

From All Saints' Day there are broad beans. Plant them at different times around Christmas, and in January, February, and early March, so that if some freeze, the others will not. When they rise above the ground, as soon as they sprout, rake them and break the first shoot. When they have six leaves, hoe them. The first to come up are the best of all and ought to be eaten the day they are shelled; otherwise they become black and sour.

If you protect sweet marjoram and violets from cold in the winter, do not take them suddenly from cold to warm or from damp to cold; if you keep them for a long time in a damp cellar in winter and suddenly put them in a dry place, you will lose them. *Et sic de contrariis similibus* [And thus from contrary effects similar things may result].

In winter, remove the dead branches of sage.

Plant sage, lavender, costmary, mint, and clary in January and February, and up until June. Sow poppies broadly. Sow sorrel at the waning of the moon, up until March and beyond.

The winter cold of December and January kills those parts of green vegetables that are out of the ground. But in February, as soon as the cold ceases, the roots send out the shoots of new and tender green vegetables. Spinach comes up fifteen days later.

In February, savory and sweet marjoram taste as if they are almost ready to eat. They are sown at the waning of the moon, and they take only eight days to come up. Savory lasts only until the feast of St. John the Baptist.

Plant trees and vines, and sow white cabbages and round cabbages, at the waning of the moon. Note that rooted cuttings bear
shoots the same year they are planted.

Spinach, which comes up in February, has long, scalloped leaves
like oak leaves, and it grows in clumps like greens. You must blanch
the leaves and then cook them well. Beets come up later.

Raspberries and raspberry bushes are suitable for planting in
March. Graft them at the waning of the moon.

Plant houseleeks from March until the feast of St. John the
Baptist.

Sow violets and gillyflowers in March, or plant them out on St.
Remi's Day. When frosts are imminent, replant them in pots some-
time when the moon is waning so they can be put under cover and

protected from the cold in a cellar or storeroom. During the day, put them out in the air or in the sun, and water them early enough that the water will be drunk and the earth dry before you put them under cover; never put them away wet in the evening.

Plant beans and break the first stem, or hoe them, as I said before.

Parsley that is sown on the eve of the feast of the Annunciation comes up in nine days.

Plant fennel and sweet marjoram at the waning of the moon in March or April. Sweet marjoram likes richer soil than violets, and if it has too much shade, it becomes yellow. When it is well rooted, pull it up in clumps and replant it in roomy pots. Branches that are cut, stuck in the earth, and watered take root and grow.

Soil fertilized with cow and sheep dung is better than that fertilized with horse manure.

Sweet violets and Armenian violets don't require cover or shelter. The Armenian violet doesn't produce flowers until the second year; but gardeners who have had it in the ground for a year sell it, and wherever it is replanted it flowers.

Sow sorrel and basil at the waning of the moon in January and February, up until March. If you want to replant sorrel that is more than a year old, you must replant it with all the soil that is around its roots. It takes skill to pick it: always take the large leaves and leave the little leaves that are above them to grow. If by chance all the leaves are picked, cut the stems right down to the ground, and new growth will come up.

Sow parsley, hoe it, and remove little stones. That sown in August is the best, for it never goes to seed and is good all year long.

Lettuce should be sown. It comes up quickly, and it grows very thickly. Because of this, pull up some here and there by the roots so the others will have space to grow full. The seed of French lettuce is black. The seed of Avignon lettuce, brought by Monsieur de la Rivière, is whiter. This is more tender than the French lettuce, and it is the best. The seed is gathered as it is set by successive heads.

Lettuce is not firmly rooted. When you want to eat it, pull it up root and all.

Gourds [squash]: The pips are the seeds. Soak them for two days, then sow them, and without watering them let them grow until they show above ground. Then water only the base and the earth, without wetting the leaves. In April, water them gently and transplant them, a handbreadth or a half-foot deep, with a half-foot from each gourd to the next. Water the base continuously by means of a perforated water pot, hung on a stake, that has a straw or a knotted strip of cloth coming from it.

Sow beets in March. When they are ready to eat, they should be cut close to the root, for they always put out new shoots, grow, and stay green.

Sow borage and orach as above.

White cabbage and great-headed cole are the same. They are sown at the waning of the moon in March. When they have five leaves, uproot them carefully and plant them half a foot apart. Plant them to the depth of the bud, and water the base. They are eaten in June or July.

Sow round cabbages in March and transplant them in May. Roman cabbages are like round cabbages, and the seeds are somewhat similar. In both, the seed grows on a stem. Round cabbage

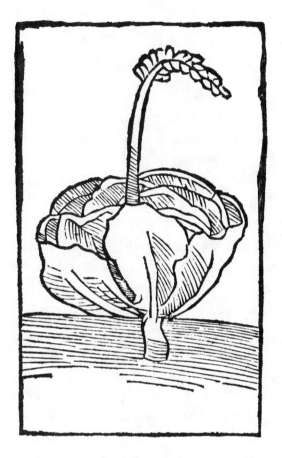

grows from the seed at the top of the middle stalk. Roman cabbage grows from the seed that comes from the bottom.

Lenten sprouts are the second growth of cabbage. They last until March, at which time they have a stronger taste; because of this they must be thoroughly boiled. At this time pull the stalks out of the ground.

If there are many ants in the garden, throw the sawdust of oak boards on the ant hill, and they will die or go away at the first rainfall, because the sawdust holds the moisture.

April, May, June, and July

Throughout the months of April and May sow the green vegetables that are eaten in June and July.

Cut the green vegetables of summer, leaving their roots in the earth. After winter, the roots put out new shoots, and you must hoe and loosen the soil around them. Sow new ones, and pick the new shoots of the old.

From April until the feast of the Magdalene is a good time to sow green vegetables. Lenten greens are sown in July up to the feast of the Magdalene, and not beyond; they are called beets. . . . When beets have sprouted they are transplanted in rows.

In April and May set out white cabbages and round cabbages that were sown in February and March. In May, one finds new beans, turnips, and radishes.

In June, on the eve of the feast of St. John the Baptist, plant parsley. Also on the eve of the feast of the Assumption of the Virgin.

When it rains in July, plant cabbages.

August and September

In August and mid-August, sow hyssop. Sow Easter cabbage at the waning of the moon; also parsley, for this won't go to seed at all.

Green vegetables, like parsley, that are in the earth send out new shoots five or six times. They can be cut above the stalk until the middle of September. After that, do not cut them at all, for the stems will rot, but strip away by hand the leaves on the outside, not those in the middle. At this time remove all seeds of green vegetables, for because the weather is cold, the seeds can't ripen. Once the seeds are stripped away and discarded, the stem puts out new greens. At this time, thin the leaves of parsley instead of cutting it.

After *Septembresse*, plant peonies, dragonwort, lily bulbs, rose bushes, and gooseberry bushes.

October and November

In October plant peas and beans a finger deep in the earth and a handbreadth from each other. Plant the biggest beans, for when they are new these prove themselves to be larger than the smaller ones can ever become. Plant only a few of them, and at each waning of the moon afterward, a few more so that if some of them freeze, the others will not. If you want to plant pierced peas, sow them in weather that is dry and pleasant, not rainy, for if rain water gets into the openings of the peas, they will crack and split in two and not germinate.

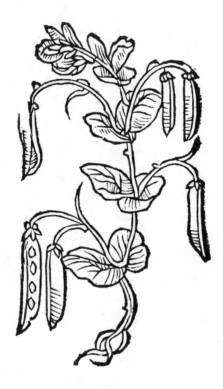

Up until All Saints' Day you can always transplant cabbages. When they are so much eaten by caterpillars that there is nothing left of the leaves except the ribs, all will come back as sprouts if they are transplanted. Remove the lower leaves and replant the cabbages to the depth of the upper bud. Do not replant the stems that are completely defoliated; leave these in the ground, for they will send up sprouts. If you replant in summer and the weather is dry, you must pour water in the hole; this is not necessary in wet weather.

If caterpillars eat the cabbages, spread cinders under the cabbages when it rains and the caterpillars will die. If you look under the leaves of the cabbages, you will find there a great collection of small white morsels in a heap. This is where the caterpillars are born, and therefore you should cut off the part with these eggs and throw it far away.

Leeks are sown in season, then transplanted in October and November.

If you want to have grapes without seeds, at the time when the vine is planted in February, during the waxing of the moon, take a grapevine with the root, split the stock in half along its length to the root, and remove the pith from each half. Then trim the stock, cover it well with dung, and bind it up all along its length with black thread. Plant it and fill the hole with earth up to the node.

If You Want to Graft a Cherry Tree

If you want to graft a cherry tree or a plum tree to a vine stock, prune the vine, then in March split it to four fingers from the end, remove the pith from both parts, make a place, and enclose the kernel of a cherry stone in this slit. With thread, tie up the vine stock, joined as I described above.

If you want to graft a vine stock onto a cherry tree, prune the vine stock, which will be planted near the cherry tree and left to root for a long time. In March, around the feast of the Annunciation of our Lady, with an auger make a hole the size of the vine stock in the cherry tree and push the vine stock through the hole and a foot beyond the cherry tree. Then stop up the hole on both sides of the cherry with clay and moss, and wind a piece of cloth around it so that no rain can come into contact with the hole. The part of the vine stock that is inside the cherry tree should have its bark peeled and removed down to the green. With the bark peeled and removed like this, the heart of the vine stock will join to the heart of the cherry. (If the bark of the vine stock is left, it will prevent this.) After doing this, leave them together for two years, and then cut the vine stock behind and below the juncture with the cherry tree.

To graft ten or twelve trees to the trunk or stump of an oak: In the month of March, around the feast of the Annunciation of our Lady, equip yourself with as many scions and various fruits as you want to have for grafting. Have the oak or tree on which you want to graft sawn through. Have your scions sharpened to a point on one side only, like a wedge, like this: ⌐. The bark on one side should be left intact, not peeled or cut into. Drive your scions between the bark and the wood of the oak, with the inner bark of the scion toward the wood and the inner bark of the oak. Then stop it up and cover it with clay, moss, and cloth, so that no rain, snow, or frost can come into contact with it.

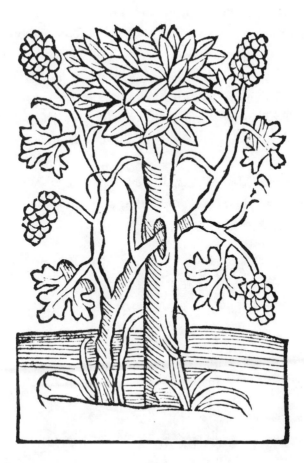

To Keep Roses in Winter

If you want to keep roses in winter, take from the rosebush little buds that are not in full bloom. Leave their stems long, and pack them together in a little wooden cask, like a compote keg, without water. Have the cask well staved in tightly bound rows so that nothing can get in or out. Fasten two large, heavy stones at both ends of this cask, and put it into a running stream.

Rosemary: Gardeners say that the seed of rosemary never grows in French soil, but if you pull off some little branches of rosemary, strip them down toward the base, hold them by the tips, and plant them, they will grow again. If you want to send rosemary branches a long distance, wrap them in waxed cloth, sew them up, anoint the outside with honey, dust them with wheat flour, and send them where you will.

I have heard Monseigneur de Berry say that in Auvergne, because they layer their cherry trees, they have fatter cherries than in France.

VI

THE HOUSEHOLD

There Are Three Kinds of Servants

Dear sister, if you want to be a housewife or instruct one of your friends in this, you should know that there are three kinds of servants. Some are engaged as helpers for a fixed period of time to do a quick job (such as porters, men with wheelbarrows, packers, and the like), or for a day or two, a week, or a season, for work that is urgent, arduous, or laborious (such as reapers, mowers,

threshers, grape harvesters, basket carriers, fullers, coopers, and the like). Others are hired for a certain amount of time because of special skills (tailors, furriers, bakers, butchers, shoemakers, and the like who do piecework). Still others are taken on as domestic servants to work by the year and live in the home. Of all these, there is not one who does not eagerly seek work and a master.

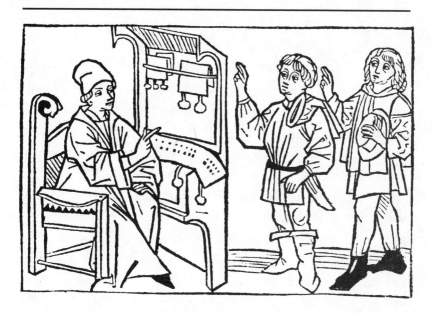

As for the first, they are needed to unload and carry burdens, and to do rough and heavy jobs. These are generally troublesome, surly, dishonest, arrogant, haughty, and quarrelsome about payment—ready to deliver insults and accusations if one doesn't pay them according to their liking when the job is done. Please, dear sister, when you have to deal with these people, ask Master Jehan the Steward, or another of your household servants, to search out and choose, or have sought and chosen, the mild-tempered ones. And always bargain with them before they start the work, so there won't be any argument afterward. What usually happens, though, is that they don't want to bargain but are ready to forge ahead with the job without coming to an agreement. They say so sweetly: "Sir, it is nothing, it is not necessary; you will pay me well, and I will be satisfied with whatever you decide." If Master Jehan engages them in this manner, when the job is done they will say: "Sir, there was more work than I thought. There was this and that to do, and a lot of running around." And they will not agree to the payment and will shout ugly and mean words. Therefore, tell Master Jehan not to put them to work, or let anyone else put them to work, without bargaining first. For those who want to earn money are your subjects before the work begins: they are compelled to be more reasonable because they need to earn money, and they fear that someone else will get the job first and they will lose the bargain and the profits. But if Master Jehan were trusting and swayed by their seductive words, and if he should happen to let them begin work without bargaining, they know very well that after they have begun anyone else would be ashamed to take on the job; and thus you would be at their mercy and they would ask for more money. And then if they aren't paid what they want, they will complain and bawl nasty and unreasonable rebuke. What is worse, they are ashamed of nothing and will give you a bad name. Because of this, it is better to dicker with them evenly and plainly beforehand to avoid any dispute.

I earnestly beg you, if the work or the business requires it, have inquiries made about how those you want to employ conduct and have conducted themselves toward others. Also, have nothing to do with people who talk back or are arrogant, haughty, mocking, or insolent—no matter what benefit or advantage you see in them or how good a bargain they would make with you. Send them away from you and your work graciously and calmly. For if they begin, you will not escape without slander or strife. Because of this, have your people hire servants and helpers who are peaceful and good natured, and pay them more, for all peace and quiet depend on dealing with agreeable servants. That is why it is said: "Whoever has to do with good servants can relax." And similarly, one could say: "Whoever has to do with surly people, his grief increases."

Concerning others—such as those who work in the vineyards, threshers, laborers, and the like, or tailors, drapers, shoemakers, butchers, farriers, makers of tallow candles (and note that for making tallow candles it is necessary to dry the wick well by the fire), spice vendors, blacksmiths, cartwrights, and the like—dear sister, I advise and pray that you always remember to tell your people that they must have peaceful folk work for them, and always bargain ahead of time, and do the accounts and pay often, without allowing long credit to build up either by tally or on paper. Although tally or account books are better than always relying on memory, for the creditors always imagine more and the debtors less, and from this are born disputes, grudges, and foul reproaches. Have your good creditors paid willingly and often what they are owed, and be kind to them so they don't change toward you, for it is not always possible to get truly peaceable people again.

As for chambermaids and house servants, who are called domestics, dear sister, so that they will obey you better and have more fear of angering you, I leave you the power and authority to have them chosen by Dame Agnes the Beguine (or some other woman whom it will please you to have in our service), to hire them, pay them,

keep them in our service, and dismiss them as you please. Nevertheless, you should speak to me privately about this and take my advice, because you are too young, and in this it is quite possible for you to be deceived by even your own people.

Be aware that of those chambermaids who are out of work, there are many who come forward, present themselves, and urgently seek masters and mistresses. Don't take any of these without first knowing where they lived before. Send some of your own people there to ask about their character—whether they talk or drink too much, how long they were there, what work they did and know how to do, whether they have lodgings or acquaintances in the town, what country and people they come from, how long they were there, and why they left. Through their past work you will find out what confidence or trust you may have in their future work. Often such women from distant parts of the country have gone into service away from home because they have been accused of some vice in their own region. For if they were faultless, they would be mistresses and not servants; and the same is true of men. If you ascertain, from what her master, mistress, neighbors, or others tell you, that a girl meets your needs, find out from her: her name and the names of her father, mother, and any other of her relatives, the place where they live, the place where she was born, and her sureties. And the day you hire her, in her presence, have Master Jehan the Steward record these things in his account book. For servants will be more afraid to make mistakes when they know that you have recorded these things so that if they leave you without permission, or if they commit some offense, you will complain about it or write to the authorities in their district, or to their friends. Nevertheless, keep in mind the adage of the philosopher called Bertram the Old, who said: "If you hire a chambermaid, or manservant, who answers you arrogantly and proudly, when she leaves she will do you injury if she can; and if she is all flattery and blandishment, don't trust her at all, for she intends to trick you in some way; but if she blushes and is quiet and full of shame when you correct her, love her as your daughter."

You Must Be Mistress of the House

K now, dear sister, that after your husband, you must be mistress of the house—master, overseer, ruler, and chief administrator—and it is up to you to keep the maidservants subservient and obedient to you, and to teach, reprove, and correct them. And so, prohibit them from lessening their worth by engaging in life's gluttony and excesses. Also, prevent them from quarreling with each other and with your neighbors. Don't let them speak ill of others, except to you and in secret, and only insofar as the offense affects your interest and to avoid harm to yourself. Forbid them to lie, to play unlawful games, to swear foully, and to speak words that suggest villainy or that are lewd or coarse, like some vulgar people who curse "the bloody bad fevers, the bloody bad work, the bloody bad day." It seems that they know well what a bloody day, a bloody week, etc. is, but they don't; they shouldn't know what a bloody thing is. Moreover, virtuous women don't know anything about it, for they are all disgusted at merely the sight of the blood of a lamb or a pigeon when someone kills it in front of them. And certainly women shouldn't speak of anything vulgar, certainly not about cunt, ass, or other private parts, for it is unseemly for women to talk of these things. I once heard of a virtuous young lady who was seated in a crowd of male and female friends. And by chance she said teasingly to the others: "You are crowding me so much that at least half of my cunt is wrinkled." And although she said it in fun and among her friends, thinking she was gallant, nevertheless, in private the other wise young ladies blamed her parents. Such ribald women sometimes say of a woman that she is a bawdy whore, and it seems that they know what "whore" or "bawdy" means; but honorable women don't know anything about it. Forbid them to use such language, for they don't know what they are saying. Don't let them take revenge, and teach them patiently. And you yourself, dear sister, be such in everything you do that they may find in you an example of all goodness.

Setting Your People to Work

Now we must speak about setting your people and servants to work at the proper times, and about the appropriate times to give them rest. Concerning this, dear sister, according to the work you have to do and the fitness of your people for the various tasks, you and Dame Agnes the Beguine (who is with you to teach you wise and mature conduct, and to serve and instruct you, and to whom I especially give the responsibility for this task) must divide up the work and give the orders, assigning one job to one and another job to another. If you tell them to do something now and your servants reply: "There is enough time; it will definitely be done," or: "It will be done early tomorrow morning," consider it forgotten—all is for nothing, and it will have to be started all over again. And also, in general, concerning what you order everyone to do, be aware that each one waits for the other to do it; it is the same as before. So you are forewarned. Tell Dame Agnes the Beguine she should see that what you want begun right away is started before her eyes. First, she should order the chambermaids, early in the morning, to sweep and clean the entrances to your house (namely, the hall and other places where people enter and stay to talk), dust the footstools, and shake out the bench cloths and coverings. And then they should similarly clean and tidy up the other rooms, and this should be done daily, as befits our social position.

Have said Dame Agnes think most especially, carefully, and diligently of your house pets, like the little dogs and birds. Also, you and the Beguine must think of the other domestic birds, for they cannot talk, and, therefore, if you have any, you must speak and think for them. Also, I say to Dame Agnes the Beguine, that when you are in the country, she is to order those who are in charge of the other beasts to look after them: Robin, the shepherd, to take care of the sheep, ewes, and lambs; Josson, the herdsman, the oxen and bulls; Arnoul, the cowherd, and Jehanneton, the dairymaid, the cows, heifers, calves, sows, pigs, and piglets; Endeline, the farmer's wife, the geese, goslings, roosters, hens, chicks, doves, and

pigeons; and the farmer's wagon man, our horses, mares, and the like. You and the said Beguine ought to let it be known to your people that you will remember it, know all about it, and have it in your heart, for then they will be more diligent. If you remember, have your people think of feeding these beasts and birds. Dame Agnes should give this work to the appropriate people.

It is up to you to have Dame Agnes the Beguine inform you of the number of sheep, ewes, and lambs you have, and have them inspected and find out how their numbers increase and decrease, and how and by whom they are cared for. And she ought to report this to you, and the two of you should see that it is written down.

If You Are in a Region
Where There Are Wolves' Dens

If you are in a region where there are wolves' dens, I will on your behalf instruct Master Jehan, your steward, or your shepherds and servants, how to kill them without striking a blow, by the following recipe.

Recipe for a powder to kill wolves and foxes: Take the root of hellebore (this is the hellebore that has a white flower) and dry the root well, but not in the sun. Remove the earth and then make a powder in a mortar. Mix into this powder a fifth part of well-ground glass and a fourth part of lily leaf. Mix and crush all this together so that it can be put through a sieve. Take honey and fresh blood in equal amounts, mix them with this powder, make a paste that is stiff and thick, form large pieces the size of a hen's egg, cover these pieces with fresh blood, and put them on stones or little tiles in places where wolves and foxes are known to go. If he wants to use an old dead animal as bait, he can prepare it two or three days beforehand and throw the powder on the decaying carcass, without forming it into pieces.

In this way you and the Beguine set some of your people to the affairs and tasks that are appropriate for them. Also, tell Master Jehan the Steward that he should send, or have sent, others to oversee your granaries, to turn and air your grains and other provisions. And if your household servants report that rats are spoiling your grain, bacon, cheese, and other supplies, tell Master Jehan that there are six ways he can kill them: first, by having a good supply of cats; second, by rat traps and mousetraps; third, by traps made of small planks propped up on sticks, which good servants make; fourth, by making cakes of fried cheese and powdered aconite and putting these in their holes where they have nothing to drink;

fifth, if you can't keep them from finding something to drink, it is well to cut little pieces of spurge and then, if they swallow them or drink they will soon swell up and die; sixth, take one ounce of aconite, two ounces of good arsenic, a quarter of a pound of pork fat, a pound of wheat flour, and four eggs. Make bread of this, cook it in the oven, cut it in strips, and fasten it down with a nail.

Take Care
of Your Furs and Dresses

But let me return to my discourse on how to put your people to
work. At suitable times you and the Beguine have your women
air, shake out, and inspect your sheets, blankets, dresses, coats,
furs, and such. Be aware, and tell your women, that to protect and
take care of your furs and dresses, you should air them often in order
to avoid the damage that the larvae of moths can do. Because such
vermin breed in the warmer periods of fall and winter and are born
in the summer, it is a good idea to put the furs and dresses in the sun
when the weather is fair and dry. If a dark, damp cloud comes and
settles on your dresses and you fold them in that condition, this air
wrapped up and folded in your garments will conceal and engender
worse vermin than before. Because of this, choose weather that will
stay fine and dry; and as soon as you see other, heavy air coming,
before it reaches you, have your dresses put under cover and shaken
to get rid of the bulk of the dust and then cleaned with a whisk of
dry twigs.

The Beguine knows well, and will tell you, that if there is any
spot of oil or other grease, this is the remedy: Take urine and heat
it until it is warm, and soak the spot in it for two days. Then,
without twisting it, squeeze out the part of the dress with the spot.
If the spot is not gone, have Dame Agnes the Beguine put it in
other urine, beat in ox gall, and do as before. Or you can do this:
Have fuller's earth soaked in lye and then put it on the spot. Let it
dry, and then rub it. If the earth doesn't come off easily, have it
moistened in lye, let it dry again, and rub until it goes away. Or, if

you don't have any fuller's earth, have ashes soaked in lye and put these well-moistened ashes on the spot. Or have very clean chicken feathers soaked in very hot water to get rid of any grease they have picked up. Wet them again in clean water, rub the spot on the dress well once more, and all the stains will go away.

If there is some stain or fading on a dress of light blue cloth, moisten a sponge in clear, clean lye, squeeze it out, draw it over the dress while rubbing the stain, and the color will come back. If there are faded spots on cloth of any other color, put very clean lye, which has not been used for boiling washing, on the spot together with ashes, and let it dry. Then rub it and the original color will come back.

To take stains out of dresses of silk, satin, camlet, silk damask, or other material: soak and wash the stain in verjuice and it will go away. Even though the dress is faded, the color will come back, although I don't really believe this.

Verjuice: At the time when the new verjuice is made, one should take a glass vial of it, without salt, and keep it, because it is useful for taking spots out of dresses and bringing back their color. It is always good, new or old.

If any of your furs or fur skins have been wet and have gotten hard, take the fur off the garment and sprinkle the fur that is hard with wine—it should be sprayed by mouth as a tailor sprays water on the part of a dress that he wants to hem. Throw flour on the watered part and let it dry for a day. Then rub the fur well and it will return to its original state.

If Your Wines Become Sick

Now let me go back to what I was talking about before and say that your steward should be aware that each week he must have your wines, verjuice, and vinegars inspected and tasted, and your grains, oils, nuts, peas, beans, and other supplies looked at.

And as for wines, if they become sick it is necessary to cure the maladies in the following manner:

If the wine is moldy, in the winter he should put the cask in the middle of a courtyard on two trestles so that the frost strikes it, and it will be cured.

If the wine is too tart, he should take a basketful of very ripe black grapes and throw them whole into the cask through the bunghole, and it will improve.

If the wine smells of sediment, he should take an ounce of powdered sermountain and an equal amount of powdered grains of paradise, put each of these in a little bag, and make a hole in it with a stick, and then hang the two little bags inside the cask on strings and plug up the bunghole well.

If the wine is oily, take twelve eggs and boil them in water until they are hard. Throw away the yellow, leave the whites and the shells together, and fry them in an iron frying skillet. Put all this hot into a little bag, pierce it with a stick (as above), and hang it in the cask on a string.

Take a large new pot and set this egg mixture above an empty trivet. When it is well cooked, cut it up into pieces, and throw them into the cask. This will cure the oiliness.

To remove the red from white wine, take a basketful of holly leaves and throw them in the cask through the bunghole.

If the wine is sour, take a pitcher of water and throw it in to separate the wine from the dregs. Then take a dishful of wheat, soak it in water, throw away the water, boil it in other water until it is just ready to burst, and remove it. If there are grains that have burst, toss them out, and throw all the rest hot into the cask. If the wine doesn't come clear with this, take a basketful of sand well washed in the Seine, throw it into the cask through the bunghole, and it will become clear.

To make a strong wine at vintage time, stop filling the cask when there is still room for two *sextiers* more, and rub all around the bunghole; then it cannot run out, and it will be stronger.

To draw wine from a barrel without letting air in, make a little hole with a drill near the bunghole, and put over this a plug of oakum the size of a small silver coin. Take two little twigs, put them crosswise on this plug, and put another plug on these twigs.

To clear muddy wine, if it is in a barrel, take out two *quartes*, then stir it with a stick or otherwise so that the dregs and all are well mixed. Then take twenty-five eggs and beat the yolks and the whites vigorously for a long time until all is perfectly clear, like water. Throw them in immediately after a quarter of a pound of beaten alum and then right away a *quarte* of clear water. Stop it up or otherwise it will run out the bunghole.

Sloth and Idleness Beget Everything Evil

Next, dear sister, have Master Jehan the Steward order Richard of the kitchen to scour, wash, clean, and do all the things that pertain to the kitchen. See that Dame Agnes the Beguine, as regards the women, and Master Jehan the Steward, as regards the men, put your people to work all around: one upstairs, one downstairs, one in the fields, the other in the village, one in the chamber, the other in the cellar or the kitchen. Send one here and the other there, every one according to his position and ability, so that each of these servants earns his or her wages doing what he or she knows and is bound to do. And if they do so, they will do well; for you know that sloth and idleness beget everything evil.

Nevertheless, dear sister, at appropriate times have them seated at table and have them eat amply of only one kind of meat, not several kinds that are fancy or dainty. Order them one nourishing beverage that is not intoxicating, either a wine that is not too strong, or something else. Bid them to eat heartily and drink well and sufficiently. It is proper that they should eat all at once, without sitting too long, without dallying over their food, pausing, or resting their elbows on the table. As soon as they begin to chat and argue, or lean on their elbows, order the Beguine to make them get up and remove their table. For common people say: "When a valet preaches at table and a horse grazes in the ford, it is time to take them away, for they have stayed long enough."

Forbid them to get drunk, and never allow a drunken person to serve or come near you, for this is dangerous. After their midday

meal, when it is time, have your people put them to work again. After their second period of work, and on feast days, let them have another meal. After that, namely, in the evening, let them be fed abundantly and amply as before. If the season requires it, see that they are warm and comfortable.

Every Evening
Before You Go to Bed

Next, your house should be closed and shut up, either by Master Jehan the Steward or the Beguine. Have one of them keep possession of the keys so that no one can go in or out without permission. Every evening before you go to bed have Dame Agnes the Beguine or Master Jehan the Steward check by the light of a candle your stores of wine, verjuice, and vinegar to see that no one has taken anything. Have your hedger or farmer find out from his people that your animals have enough fodder for the night. When you have learned from Dame Agnes the Beguine or Master Jehan the Steward that all the hearth fires are covered, give your people time and respite to rest their limbs. And make sure beforehand that each has, far from his bed, a metal candlestick for his candle, and have each wisely instructed to put it out by the mouth or the hand, and never with the shirt, just before getting into bed. Also, have each advised and instructed as to what work he must begin in the morning and when each must rise and recommence his own work. Each must be informed of this.

Nevertheless, let me advise you of two things: the one is, if you have girls or maids from fifteen to twenty years old, because at that age they are foolish and have seen little of the world, make them

sleep near you in a wardrobe or chamber, where there is, of course, no dormer or low window on the street; and they should go to bed and get up at the same time as you. And you yourself—who will be wise by this time, God willing—watch over them from nearby. The other is that if one of your servants falls sick, you yourself, neglecting everything else, think of him very kindly and charitably, and look after and care for him very lovingly while furthering his recovery.

Whoever Wants to Buy a Horse

Now I want to leave you to rest or play, and speak to you no more; amuse yourself elsewhere. I will talk to Master Jehan the Steward, who oversees our property, so that if any of our horses, plow horses as well as riding horses, are disabled, or it is necessary to buy or exchange, he will know a little about it.

Be aware, Master Jehan, that a horse should have sixteen characteristics. Three qualities of a fox: short, straight ears; good hair; and a strong tail full of hair. Four qualities of a hare: a lean head; extreme wariness; light movement; and speed. Four qualities of an ox: a wide, large, and broad chest; a large belly; large eyes that stand out from the head; and low jointedness. Three qualities of an ass: good feet; a strong backbone; and gentleness. Four qualities of a maiden: a beautiful mane; a beautiful chest; beautiful loins; and large buttocks.

Master Jehan, my friend, whoever wants to buy a horse should first of all look at the stable; for there one sees if he is in the hands of a trainer, if he is well or badly kept, if he has a good coat, and the condition of the dung. After this, when he is out of the stable, see whether his head is thin or broad, and whether his ears are short and straight, his sight good and sound, and his eyes large and protruding from his head. Then feel under the gums to determine if there are large spaces and good, broad openings, and to see that there is no slime, swelling, or canker, and that the throat passage is not in any way bruised.

Then, my friend Master Jehan, you should find out how old he is. When a horse is two, he has new teeth—white, slender, and even. In the third year, the three teeth in front change and become larger and better than the others. At four, the two teeth that are on both sides of these three change and become similar to them. At five, the others change. At six come the fangs with hollow bottoms, and there is a mark at the bottom of the hollow. At seven the edges of the hollows of the fangs are worn; there is no more hollow or mark, and they become flat and even. After that, one can't tell the age anymore.

VII

THE KITCHEN

To Keep Your Soup from Burning

When crushing spices and bread for sauces and thick soups, grind the spices first and take them out of the mortar. In this way you won't lose anything because the bread that you pound afterward takes up what is left of the spices.

Do not strain the spices and thickeners you put in soups. Sauces, however, will be clearer and more pleasant if you do so.

Generally, all soups will boil over onto the fire until you put into the pot salt and fat, which prevent this.

Peas, beans, or other stews won't stick to the bottom of the pot if the pieces of burning wood don't touch the base of the pot when it is over the fire.

To keep your soup from burning, stir it often, pressing your spoon against the bottom of the pot so that it won't stick there. As soon as you notice that it is sticking, stop stirring it, take it off the fire immediately, and put it into another pot.

To get the burnt taste out of soups, take a fresh pot and put your soup in it. Then take a little leaven, tie it in a white cloth, and throw it into your pot. Leave it there only a short time.

To make all soups less salty without adding or taking out anything, take a very white cloth, put it on your pot, and turn it over often. The pot must be kept far away from the fire.

To take salt out of butter, melt butter in a dish on the fire, and the salt will fall to the bottom of the bowl. This salt is good for soup. The rest of the butter remains sweet. Another way is to put your salted butter in fresh water, knead and pound it with your hands, and the salt will stay in the water.

Note that flies will not seek out a horse that is smeared with butter or old salted grease.

The best broth is made from the jowl of an ox, rinsed two or three times in water and then boiled and well skimmed.

Cooks distinguish between sticking and larding. Sticking means to stick with cloves, and larding means to lard with pork fat.

The Right Kind of Eel

The right kind of eel has a small head; skin that is fine, lustrous, wavy, and sparkling; a large body; and a white belly. The other kind has a large head, a brownish yellow belly, and thick, brown skin.

The soft roe of pike is better than the hard, unless you want to make rissoles, which are made of hard roe *ut patet in tabula* [so that it lies open on the table].

March is the season for shad.

Trout season lasts until September. The white ones are good in winter and the reddish ones in summer. The tail is the best part of a trout, and the head is the best part of a carp.

A carp with scales that are white, not yellow or reddish, is from good water. If it has large, protruding eyes and the roof of the mouth is soft and even, it is fat.

If you want to carry a live carp around all day, wrap it up in wet hay and carry it with the stomach up in a leather bag or a sack, without giving it air.

It is dangerous to eat carp that is not well cooked.

Plaice are smooth to the touch, dab are the opposite.

In Paris, the goose sellers fatten their geese with the finest meal, not flour or bran, but the coarse-ground flour that is in between, called *gruyaulx* or *recoppes*. They mix this meal and oats, in equal amounts, with a little water, so that the mixture holds together and is thick like paste, and they put it in a four-footed trough, with water on the side. They give the geese fresh litter every day, and in fifteen days they are fat. In addition, the litter makes them keep their feathers clean.

To mortify capons and hens, you must bleed them by the throat and immediately put them in a pail of very cold water to die. In this way you will in one day make them as gamey as if they had been dead for two days.

When mallards are all the same size, the young can be distinguished from the old by the quills on the wings, which are more supple on the young ones. River mallards have fine black claws and red feet, while those from the farmyard have yellow feet. The crown of the beak (that is to say, the upper part) is green throughout. Sometimes they have a white ring around the neck at the throat. They have wavy feathers.

Ringdoves are good in winter. You can tell the old ones because the middle feathers of their wings are uniformly black. The middle wing feathers of the young ones a year old are ash colored, and the rest of their feathers are black.

Partridges with feathers that are like those of a sparrow hawk—tightly closed, orderly, well joined, and well attached to the flesh—

have been freshly killed. Those whose feathers are raised at an uphill angle coming out of the flesh and in disarray have been dead for some time. You can tell this by pulling the feathers of the rump.

You can tell if a rabbit is fat by feeling a tendon or the neck between the two shoulders. If there is thick fat on the large tendon, you will detect it there. You can tell if he is tender by breaking one of his back legs.

You can tell the age of a hare by the number of holes under the tail, one hole per year.

It is said that one should kill male pigs in November and female pigs in December, for this is their season. That is why one speaks of February hens, for example.

Good cheese has six properties. Not Argus, not Helen, not Mary Magdalene, but Lazarus and like Martinus, answering in a pontifical manner:

Not like Helen, white,
Not like the Magdalene, crying,
Not like Argus,
But without eyes,
And also heavy
Like an ox of size.
It resists the thumb,
And is covered with scales,
Not white, not weepy, but blind,
Firm, and weighty,
With a crusty rind.

Take Your Chickens
and Cut Their Throats

Stuffed poultry: Take your chickens and cut their throats. Scald them and pluck them, being careful not to tear the skin. Parboil them. Take a tube, push it between the skin and the flesh, and blow the chicken up. Cut it between the two shoulders, without making too large a hole, and pull out the innards, leaving the thighs, wings, neck with all the head, and feet with the skin.

To make the stuffing, take mutton, veal, pork, and the dark meat of chicken, all raw, and chop them up. Pound them in a mortar

with raw eggs, good rich cheese, good spice powder, a little saffron, and salt to taste. Fill the chicken and truss the hole. With what is left of the stuffing, make balls like little lumps of woad, and cook them in beef broth or boiling beef water with plenty of saffron. Don't boil them too hard or they will fall apart. Then put them on a very thin spit and glaze them with a great many egg yolks beaten up with a little saffron. If you want green glaze, bray greens, then well-beaten egg yolks, and run them through a strainer for greens. With this, glaze the chicken when it is cooked, and the balls as well, holding your spit in the pot with the glaze and throwing the glaze all along it. Put the spit back on the fire two or three times, so that your glaze will stick. Be careful not to let the glaze get too close to the fire or it will burn.

A Dish for Unexpected Guests

A meat dish to make quickly for supper when guests drop in unexpectedly, and there is nothing else in the house: For ten dishes, take twenty long slices of cold dinner meat and beef, small like slices of bacon, and fry them in fat in a pan on the fire. Take the yolks of six eggs and a little white wine, and beat them together until you are tired. Combine this with the juice of the meat and old verjuice (new verjuice will make it turn). Boil this mixture without the meat, and then set it out in dishes along with two strips of meat per dish. When there is not enough meat to go around, some people dish up the broth and set before four people a platter with five slices of meat, and the broth with it.

Beverages for Sick People

To make sweet barley water, take some water and boil it. Then for each *sextier* of water add an ample bowl of barley, with or without the hulls, two *parisis* worth of liquorice, and some figs, and let it boil until the barley bursts. Strain it in two or three cloths. Put a lot of crystallized sugar in each cup. Afterward, this barley is good

to give to chickens to fatten them up. Note that the good liquorice is the youngest, and when cut it is bright green; the old is colorless, dead, and dry.

Flemish broth: Boil a pot of water. Then for each bowl beat four egg yolks with white wine. Pour this in a thin stream into your water, stirring well. Add salt to taste. When it is well boiled, take it off the fire. When making one bowl for one sick person, use five eggs.

Take Five Hundred New Walnuts

his is the way to make compote. It should be begun on St. John's Day, which is the twenty-fourth of June. First, around that time, take five hundred new walnuts, being careful that the shells and the kernels are not yet formed, and that the shells are not yet too hard or too soft. Peel them all around, make holes through

them in three places or in the form of a cross, put them to soak in Seine or well water, and change the water every day. Let them soak ten or twelve days (they will turn black) until there is no bitterness when you chew them. Then boil them awhile in sweet water, for as long as it takes to say a *miserere*, or until they are neither too hard nor too soft. After this, throw out the water and put them in a sack to drain. Take honey, a *sextier* or as much as will thoroughly cover them, and melt it until it is runny and foamy. When it is cooled to lukewarm again, add the nuts. Leave them two or three days, then drain them. Take as much of your honey as will cover them, put it on the fire, bring it once to a rapid boil, skim it, and take it off the fire. In each of the holes in the nuts stick a clove on one side and a little piece of cut ginger in the other. When the honey is luke-warm, put the nuts in it and then turn them two or three times a day. After four days take them out and boil the honey again; if there is not enough, add more. Boil it, skim it, boil it, and then add the nuts. Do this every week for a month. Then leave them in an earthenware pot or a cask, and turn them once a week.

Around All Saints' Day, take large turnips, peel them, and cut them into quarters. Parboil them, and then take them out of the water and put them in cold water to soften. Drain them. Melt honey as for the nuts. Be careful not to cook the turnips too long.

On All Saints' Day, take as many carrots as you wish, pare them, cut them into pieces, and cook them like the turnips. (Carrots are the red roots that they sell by the handful at the market Les Halles, a half-sou a handful.)

Take choke pears and cut them into quarters. Don't peel them. Cook them the same as the turnips, no more and no less.

When gourds [squash] are in season, take the medium-ripe ones, peel them, remove the insides, quarter them, and cook them like the turnips.

When peaches are in season, take the hardest, peel them, and cut them up.

Around St. Andrew's Day, take roots of parsley and fennel, cut off the tops, and chop them up into little pieces. Split the fennel through and take out the hard centers. Don't throw away this part of the parsley, however. Proceed as before.

When all your sweetmeats are ready, prepare what goes with them by the following recipe: For five hundred nuts take a pound of mustard seed, a half pound of anise seed, three-quarters of a pound

of fennel seed, three-quarters of a pound of coriander seed, three-quarters of a pound of caraway seed (this is a seed that one eats in sweetmeats), and reduce all to a powder. Then grind all this in a mustard mill, steep it thickly in very fine vinegar, and put it in an earthenware pot.

Take a half pound of horseradish (this is a root the herbalists sell), pare it well, cut it up as small as you can, grind it in a mustard mill, and steep it in vinegar.

Take an eighth of a pound of clove wood (called clove stalk), an eighth of a pound of cinnamon, an eighth of a pound of pepper, an eighth of a pound of Mecca ginger, an eighth of a pound of nutmeg, an eighth of a pound of grains of paradise, and make a powder of all these.

Take half an ounce of dried and beaten saffron of Ort, and one ounce of sandalwood (this is a wood that spice sellers sell; it is called "the sandalwood from which they sell knife handles"). Then take a pound of good honey, heavy and white, and melt it over the fire. When it is well cooked and clarified, let it settle. Then strain it and cook it again, and if it sends up scum, you must strain it again; if not, let it cool. Moisten your mustard with equal amounts of good wine and vinegar, and put it in the honey. Moisten your powdered spices with wine and vinegar and put them in honey and hot wine. Boil your sandalwood a little and add the saffron with the other ingredients and a handful of coarse salt.

Then take two pounds of fresh grapes—called grapes from Digne, which are small and have no stones or pits—pound them well in a mortar, and soak them in good vinegar. Run them through a strainer and add them to the other ingredients. If you add four or five *pintes* of unfermented wine or boiled wine, the sauce will be even better.

To make a quince confection: Take quinces and peel them. Then cut them into quarters and remove the eyes and the seeds. Boil them in good red wine and then run them through a strainer. Take honey, boil it for a long time, and skim it. Add your quinces, stir well, and boil until the honey is reduced by at least half. Then throw in powder of hippocras and stir until it is thoroughly cold. Cut it into pieces and keep it.

Hippocras: To make hippocras powder, take a quarter of a pound of very fine cinnamon, chosen by biting it; an eighth of a pound of cinnamon powder; one ounce of choice, fine, white Mecca ginger; one ounce of grains of paradise; a sixth part of nutmeg and galingale combined; and beat them all together. When you want to make hippocras, take an ample half ounce of this powder and mix it with a half pound of sugar and a *quarte* of wine, Paris measure. Note that the mixture of powder and sugar is called "duke's powder."

To make a *quarte* or a *quarteron* of hippocras by the measure of Béziers, Carcassonne, or Montpellier, take five *drames* of fine, clean cinnamon; three *drames* of pared choice white ginger; a *drame* and a quarter altogether of cloves, grains of paradise, mace, galingale, nutmeg, spikenard—more of the first and less of each of the others, in descending order. Make a powder and mix with it a pound and an eighth, by the heavy weight, of rock sugar ground and mixed with the other spices. Put sugar in a large dish and melt it in wine on the fire, mixing in the powder. Then put the mixture in the straining bag and strain it until it returns to clear red. Note that the flavor of sugar and cinnamon ought to predominate.

To make thick wine for sauces: Take as much unpressed wine as you like (either white or red) from the vat or cask, put it in an earthen vessel, and boil it moderately over a bright and smokeless fire of very dry logs. Remove the scum with a pierced scoop made of wood, not iron. If the year's vintage is green, it should be boiled until the

wine is reduced by two-thirds; if it is ripe, by three-fourths. Then put it in a tub or other clean wooden vessel to cool. When it has cooled, put it in a wine vessel. It will be better the third or fourth year than the first. Keep it in a place with a moderate temperature, not hot or cold. Retain a little vessel of this boiled wine so you can always replenish the cask, for it should be full at all times.

Wafers are made in four ways: One method is to beat eggs in a bowl, add salt and wine, throw in flour, and moisten all this together. Then cook the dough a little bit at a time in two irons. Each time, put between the irons as much dough as there is in a slice of cheese, press the irons firmly together, and cook one side and then the other. If the dough doesn't come out of the irons easily, first smear them with oil or fat on a little cloth.

The second method is like the first, but one adds cheese. Stretch the dough as if making a tart or a pie, put the slices of cheese in the middle, and cover up the two ends. The cheese is cooked between the two pieces of dough.

The third kind are filtered wafers, so-called only because the dough is clearer, like pancake batter. It is mixed with finely grated cheese.

The fourth kind is made of flour kneaded with water, salt, and wine; it has no eggs or cheese.

The wafer makers offer another kind called big sticks, which are made of flour kneaded with eggs that have been beaten together with ginger powder. These are the size of chitterlings, and they are cooked between two irons.

To make candied orange peel: Divide the skin of an orange into five pieces and with a knife scrape out the pith that is inside. Soak the pieces for nine days in good, sweet water, changing the water every day. Then boil them quickly, letting the water bubble up just once, spread them out on a cloth, and leave them to become thoroughly dry. Put them in a pot, cover them completely with honey, boil them over a low fire, and skim. When you think the honey is cooked, test it by dropping a little bit into a dish of water. If it spreads, it is not cooked; but if it holds together, it is cooked. Then take out the orange peels one after the other, make a layer, and sprinkle powdered ginger on them. Then make another layer and do the same until they are all used up. Leave for a month or more before eating.

VIII

OTHER SMALL
MATTERS

To make water for washing hands at table: Boil sage, then strain the water and cool it until it is a little more than lukewarm. Or use chamomile, marjoram, or rosemary boiled with orange peel. Bay leaves are also good.

Drinks seasoned with sage: To make a cask of sage-flavored liquid, take two pounds of sage, clip off the stems, and put the leaves in the cask. Have a half ounce of cloves in a little cloth bag hung in the cask on a small cord. You can also put in a half ounce of bay, or an eighth of a pound of Mecca ginger, an eighth of a pound of long pepper, and an eighth of a pound of bay. When you want to make sage-flavored drinks at table in winter, have a ewer of sage water and pour it over white wine in a goblet.

To make white wine red at table: In summer, take the red flowers that grow in wheat, which are called *perseau, neele,* or *passe rose,* and dry them so they can be made into powder. Secretly throw them into a glass with the wine, and it will turn red.

To make salt white: Take a *pinte* of rock salt and three *pintes* of water. Put them on the fire long enough to melt together, then strain in a tablecloth, towel, or straining cloth. Put the mixture on the fire, and bring it to a good boil and skim it. Boil it long enough so that it is thus completely dry and the little bubbles that have thrown out water are all evaporated. Then remove the salt from the pan and spread it out on a tablecloth in the sun to dry.

To write on paper a letter that no one will see unless the paper is heated: Take sal ammoniac and melt it by moistening it with water. Then write with this and let it dry. This will last about eight days.

To make birdlime: Peel holly when the sap is running (usually from May to August). Boil the bark in water until the thin skin on it separates, then peel it off. Wrap what is left in leaves of elder, dwarf

elder, or other large leaves, and put it in a cold place (in a cellar, underground, or in a cold dung hill) for nine days or more, until it is decayed. Then pound it like cabbage porray and form it into cakes like woad. Wash the cakes one at a time and break them into pieces like wax. Make sure you don't wash them too much the first time, or in water that is hard. After this, you can break it all up and mold it in your hands under swiftly running water. Keep it in a well-covered pot. If you want to make it runnier, heat a little oil, melt your birdlime in it, and then glue your line. Another kind of birdlime is made from wheat.

If you want to keep roses red: Take a dozen buds, gather them together like a ball, wrap them in flax, and tie them with thread. Make as many of these balls as you need for the roses you want to preserve, put them in a pot made of earth of Beauvais (don't use any other kind), and fill the pot with verjuice. Replenish the verjuice as it is consumed, making sure it is mature. When you want the roses to open, take them out of the flax, put them in warm water, and let them soak a little.

To keep roses in another way: Take all the buds you want and put as many as you can in a bottle made of Beauvais earth. Then take the finest sand, put as much as you can into the bottle, and stop it up so tightly that nothing can get in or out. Put the bottle in running water. A rose will keep for a whole year in this way.

To make rose water without an alembic: Take a barber's basin, stretch a kerchief over the mouth, and fasten it, covering the basin completely, like a drum. Put your roses on the kerchief and above them set the bottom of another basin containing hot cinders and live coals.

To make rose water without an alembic or fire: Take two glass basins and do as above, but instead of cinders and coals, set everything in the sun, whose heat will make the water.

Roses of Provins are the best for putting in dresses, but you should dry them and in mid-August sift them so that the worms fall through the holes of the sieve. Then scatter them on the dresses.

To make red rose water: Fill a glass vial half with good rose water and half with young red rose petals that have the white cut away from the tip. Leave nine days and nights in the sun and then pour.

How to make caged birds lay eggs, sit on them, and raise their young: In the aviary at Hesdin (which is the largest in this realm), in the king's aviary at St. Pol, and in Sir Hugues Aubryot's aviary, they never get birds to brood and raise little ones. In Charlot's aviary they do, however. The problem in the first three places is that the little birds are fed hemp seed, which is hot and dry, and they have very little to drink. At Charlot's aviary, however, the birds are given fresh chickweed, sow thistle, or creeping thistle soaked in water that is always fresh because it is changed three times a day, and in dishes of lead. The sow thistle and chickweed are green; the stems of the creeping thistle have been well soaked in water; and the dishes also contain hemp seed that has been pressed, hulled, and soaked in water.

The birds are given carded wool and feathers for making their nests, and thus I have seen caged turtledoves, linnets, and goldfinches lay eggs and raise their young.

Also, they should be given caterpillars, little worms, flies, spiders, grasshoppers, butterflies, and new hemp seed with herbs, moistened and soaked. Spiders, grasshoppers, and such things are soft to the tender beaks of little birds—this is the kind of food peacocks feed their chicks. When hens sit on peacock eggs with their own, all the eggs hatch at the same time; but the little peacocks cannot live long because their beaks are too soft for the food

134

the hens search for. Also, chickens live on wheat, or meal and bran soaked in slops, which is not proper food for peacocks. Yet when hens are given the best sifted wheat, they shake it to find worms and flies.

At the end of April, go out and look for branches with three forks, nail them to the wall, and cover them with other greens; and there, in the fork, the birds make their nest.

To cure a toothache: Take an earthenware pot with a lid. The pot should be tightly sealed with clay, and the lid should have a hole in the middle. Or take a lidless pot covered with a trencher that has a hole in the middle. Fill the pot with water, put sage or other herbs in it, and set it to boil. Take off your clothes and get into bed. With your head well covered, position your open mouth over the hole so you can breathe the steam passing through it. Keep yourself well covered.

To make sand to put in an hourglass: Take the silt that falls when they saw large tombs from black marble. Boil it well in wine like a piece of meat, skim it, and put it in the sun to dry. Boil, skim, and dry it nine times, and it will be good.

Poison for killing a stag or a wild boar: Take the root of wolfsbane, pound it in a mortar, put it in a sack or small cloth, and squeeze it to get the juice. Put this juice in a dish in the sun, and at night keep it under cover and dry so that no water or other moisture can touch it. Move it in and out of the heat until it is glutinous and formed like thickened wax, and then put it in a tightly closed box. When you want to shoot an arrow, put some of it between the barbs and the iron socket, so that the beast will be struck down when it hits and makes contact with the flesh. If the iron is not smeared in this way, when it enters the skin of the beast, the ointment stays there and the strike will be worth nothing.

Medicine to cure the bite of a dog or other mad beast: Take a crust of bread and write the following: + *bestera* + *bestie* + *nay* + *brigonay* + *dictera* + *sagragan* + *es* + *domina* + *fiat* + *fiat* + *fiat.*

To turn a boar into a proper wild boar: Take a boar that is about two years old and in the month of May or June have him castrated. In boar-hunting season, have him hunted, killed, and dismembered like a wild boar. Or do this: Take an ordinary hog that has been seared, cook it in half water half wine, and serve it on a platter with this broth together with turnips and chestnuts.

To remove water from wine: Put the watered wine in a cup. Place one end of a cotton thread at the bottom of the cup. Hang the other end of the thread over the edge, outside and below the cup, and you will see that the water will drip out colorless at this end. When the water has all dripped out, the wine will drip out red. It seems that one could do the same with a cask of wine.

To make a liquid for marking linen: Take axle grease (the dirt at both ends of the axle tree of a wagon), add ink, combine oil and vinegar, and boil all this together. Then heat your marker, moisten it in this mixture, and set it on your linen.

If you want to make good tinder for lighting your fire with a fire steel: Take the fungus of old walnut trees, put it in a pot full of very strong lye (whole or in pieces the size of two fingers, as you prefer), and boil it continuously for at least two days and a night. If you don't have lye, take good ashes, put them in the water, and make buck-ashes. Then set the fungus to boil in this for the amount of time stated above, and keep filling it with as much as boils away, using lye if you are boiling it in lye, and water if you are boiling it with buckashes. No matter what you boil it in, if you add urine, it will be better. When it has thus boiled, strain it, and then rinse it in good clean water to wash it. Then put it in the sun to dry, or in the chimney, far from the fire so it won't burn, for it must dry evenly and slowly. When it is dry and you want to use it, beat it with a mallet or a staff until it is cleaned out. When you want to light a fire, take a piece the size of a pea, put it on your flint stone, and you will have fire immediately. And you need only blow on the wick to light a candle. Keep it clean and dry.

To make three pintes *of ink:* Take galls and gum, two ounces of each, and three ounces of copperas. Crush the galls and soak them three days. Then boil them in three *quartes* of rain water, or water from a still pool. When they have boiled enough and the water is almost half-boiled away (i.e., no more than three *pintes* are left), take it off the fire, add the copperas and gum, and stir it until it is cold. Then put it in a cold, damp place. After three weeks it spoils.